D1284709

D.I.Y.
Magic

D.I.Y. Magic

A Book of Mind Hacks

ANTHONY ALVARADO

SOUVENIR PRESS

Copyright © 2012, 2015 by Anthony Alvarado

First published in Great Britain in 2015 by Souvenir Press Ltd,
43 Great Russell Street, London WC1B 3PD

Published by arrangement with Perigee, an imprint of Penguin Publishing Group,
a division of Penguin Random House LLC

First published by Floating World Comics 2012

The right of Anthony Alvarado to be identified as the author
of this work has been asserted in accordance with section 77
of the Copyright, Designs and Patents Act, 1988

All rights reserved.
No part of this publication may be reproduced, stored in a retrieval system
or transmitted, in any form or by any means, electronic, mechanical, photocopying,
or otherwise, without the prior permission of the Copyright owner.

While the author has made every effort to provide accurate telephone numbers,
Internet addresses, and other contact information at the time of publication, neither the
publisher nor the author assumes any responsibility for errors, or for changes that occur after
publication. Further, the publisher does not have any control over and does not assume
any responsibility for author or third-party websites or their content.

Neither the publisher nor the author is engaged in rendering professional advice or
services to the individual reader. The ideas, procedures, and suggestions contained in
this book are not intended as a substitute for consulting with your physician. All matters regarding
your health require medical supervision. Neither the author nor the publisher shall be liable or
responsible for any loss or damage allegedly arising from any information or suggestion in this book

ISBN 9780285643208

Text design by Laura K. Corless

Printed and bound in Denmark by Nørhaven

FOR SARAH

Perhaps the immobility of the things around us is imposed on them by our certainty that they are themselves and not anything else, by the immobility of our mind confronting them.

—Marcel Proust, *Swann's Way*

CONTENTS

Contents

Contents

INTRODUCTION

What I Talk About When I Talk About Magic

Superstition is rooted in a much deeper and more sensitive layer of the psyche than skepticism.

—Johann Wolfgang von Goethe

TECHNIQUE

Read this book and try the experiments presented here. Change them as you see fit. You are the one in charge; these are just beginning points. Reading this book with an open mind will change the way you think about yourself, about creativity, and about the world. Think of this like you would a travel guidebook to, say, Guatemala or the Czech Republic. If you buy the book, you better plan on actually going there, right? This is not a book merely to be read; it is a book to be lived!

TOOLS REQUIRED

1 copy of the book in your hands
An open mind
Bonus: It's nice to have a notebook to take notes. You will get a lot
of cool ideas doing these experiments.

TIME REQUIRED

288 pages

RESULT

A radically original arsenal of ways to think, perceive, and experience the world.

⚜

When I talk about magic, I'm not fucking around. It isn't a joke or
a trick. I'm talking about real techniques that most people are
capable of trying out if they let themselves.

Most people, however, don't.

Magic is taboo. It's considered the realm of flakes, hippies, and
drug-addled softies—a waste of time.

Introduction

But the good stuff always is.

Dig a little deeper with me, dear reader, and I will point you in the direction of uncharted waters. Here there be dragons.

I have tried to summarize what this is all about dozens of times and each time used a different metaphor, because all fall short. Imagine trying to describe the act of swimming to someone who has never seen a body of water larger than that held in a cup. Or trying to describe music to the uninitiated, not just hearing music but playing music . . . where to begin? How to come up with something not feeble and academic like: It is a series of rhythmic tones that are pleasing to the ear? Ha!

No, the best thing to be done would be to lay out simple and straightforward instructions on how to whittle a flute, how to build a drum, or how to whistle and clap your hands, and from these rudimentary recipes enterprising readers would be able to find their own way. Mere description would be meaningless.

In the same way, I have laid out some guideposts in this book, some simple instruments that you are welcome to construct for your own amusement. If any of these ideas strike you as poppycock, skip them. Use what you can use and throw away the rest.

What is magic? It is the fine and subtle art of driving yourself insane! No, really, it is just that. It is a con you play on your own brain. It is the trick of letting yourself go crazy—I do believe that when it's done right, the magus treads the same sacred and profane ground where walks the madman. It is, however, possible for the modern magician to enter that realm and return with knowledge and, yes, power.

That said, I must warn you that these arts should be practiced only by those who are sound of mind. Like a powerful drug, the visions and experiences that are open to the initiate are not vouchsafed for all. As with trying anything new, use common sense, be safe, and don't take on more than you can handle. If you can't afford to lose your mind a bit, then please put this book back on the shelf and walk away. . . .

Still here? Good. Having shared that caveat, I will also say that this book does not dabble in black magic. That is the harnessing or deal brokering with nonhuman entities of one shade or another. If that's what you're looking for, you're barking up the wrong tree and should consult a less straightforward grimoire than this one.

That is not to say that the practitioner of the arts described here won't meet strange and compelling creatures and characters along the way. However, I believe that at some level these entities are subconscious structures of our own making. Does this make them any less powerful or capricious? In my experience, no.

In short, rather than advertise this as a book of magic, it could just as well have been labeled a book of psychology hacking or a creativity cookbook. Think of it as jail breaking the smartphone of your mind, teaching it to do things that its basic programming was never set up for. Advanced self-psychology.

Introduction

Had enough analogies and ready to move on to the main course? Wait, here is one last story; it is the same story that all stories are made of, the only story. All are endless variations of this: The hero leaves the world of common day and enters a region of supernatural wonder, fabulous forces are encountered, and a decisive victory is won. The hero returns from this mysterious adventure with the power to bestow boons on his fellow man. This book beckons you to take the hero's journey.

The truth is we have all practiced a form of magic at one time, when we were children seeing images in the passing clouds. Remember lying on your back watching faces appear in the sky? A puff of cumulus becomes the eye of some creature that melts into an alligator's nose and then becomes fantastic dogs, castles, angels, cartoons of people and animals that waltz from one form to another. Images can also be seen in the hot coals of a fire, in the grain of wood beams, and on the surface of rippling water. The phenomenon is surely the reason why primitive man saw himself surrounded on all sides by the elemental spirits of all things—the sprites, nymphs, dryads, and sylphs of forest, river, and fire. And wasn't he richer for it? Now of course we know better! But I propose these same faculties now lie dormant within us.

The deceptively simple exercises in this tome are designed to help us beginners born into the modern age of reason set aside the rational web of what we already *know* and allow us to *see*. The techniques for approaching this state of seeing are infinite. Some work better than others and some of the best have become codified over the centuries, like scrying with tea leaves, or tarot card readings, or prognostication by the stars. These are the familiar paths to magic. But do not be misled; they are not the only paths in the forest. And with vigor and a machete, you can hew your own trail.

The old paths all bring us to the same place: a state of transcendent awareness. The historian and philosopher Mircea Eliade believed it was the foundation of all rites of magic, from the Siberian shaman preparing to descend into the underworld in search of a lost soul to the Aborigine who walks into dreamtime to see what must be done to ensure a prosperous hunting season. Today, it is the work of the artist, the poet, all those who create, as well as the underpinnings of every hero, from Orpheus to Harry Potter.

But who is to say that one method of enchantment or entrancement is better than any other? Singing, chanting, drumming, and dancing are effective, but there is no magical law established that says the dancing must be done to tribal drums as opposed to, say, a DJ spinning 45s, or that magic will work only if the practitioner is wearing animal skins and bird feathers but not sneakers and a cotton hoody. What the Australian Aborigine elder and the Tungusic shaman have in their psychic endeavors is the support of the community in its inherent belief structures. This is the biggest obstacle the modern practitioner faces; most of the world doesn't believe magic is something to be taken seriously, and therefore the modern practice of magic demands an eccentric and confident personality who doesn't give a fig what others think.

Again and again we find that the art of magic lies in the recognition of the parallels between the self and the world. Science is devoted to breaking things down. To making everything into smaller and smaller parts. Magic works in the opposite direction. The fantastic tableaux of faces and actions, beasts and palaces visible in the clouds of your childhood were nothing but a mirror of your mind.

This book is intended to be merely a signpost showing the trailheads of a dozen or so portals that will take you there, to a path that returns to the imagination of childhood, to a path that will set you off on the hero's journey. Be warned that everything that comes after—the region you go to, the forces you encounter, the victory and what you do with it when you return—are all up to you. I would also like to humbly say that I'm not the first to tread these strange hallways. I follow in the steps of the Dadaists, the surrealists, the poets, the beatniks . . . et cetera ad nauseam. I am particularly indebted to the work of C. G. Jung.

As with any versatile art, the applications are limitless. I hope the following essays will be of particular interest to artists, musicians, writers, and all those who are chasing the muse. Here are some keys that open doors to imagination, creativity, and yes, magic.

LEXICON

A few notes on the terminology used in this book.

spell, experiment, technique, exercise: I employ these terms fairly interchangeably. *D.I.Y. Magic* consists of thirty-six chapters, each one explaining a different activity that you can try yourself. Sometimes I refer to the activity as an experiment, sometimes as a spell, sometimes as an exercise. While all of these terms denote slightly different things, I use them interchangeably here because they are all equally valid. You can think of these as psychological experiments, as philosophical exercises, or as magical spells. Indeed I encourage you to try to think of them from as many different angles as possible. However, simply be aware that there is no real difference between a spell, a technique, a thought experiment, and so on. Is it a spell that you cast upon the world or upon yourself? They are both the same— that is the secret. By changing the way you perceive the world, you change your world. This is magic.

bibliomancy: Gaining insight by randomly reading a passage from a book. See **divination**.

cantrip: While many of the spells in this book take a bit of preparation to try, a cantrip is any spell that is very quick and easy to do. These are the spells that you could try out the moment you finish reading the section on them—for example, bibliomancy, ornitho-mancy, the cloak of invisibility, the coin trick, and power stance.

divination: An attempt to gain knowledge and insight to a question by looking at something that has nothing to do with that question. See **ornithomancy.**

hypnagogic: The imagery you see as you are falling asleep. Greek for "leading to sleep."

Ludditism: Rejection of modern technology.

magus: A person learned in magic. If you read this book and try out these techniques, I would consider you a budding magus. Inter-changeable with *magician* and a bunch of other terms. I use *magus* because it is slightly unfamiliar and so has less cultural baggage. Say-ing *wizard* immediately conjures up images of a bearded guy wearing a pointed hat with stars and moons on it. Which, come to think of it, is actually pretty damn cool!

manifestation: Creating something in reality by thinking about it first. Everything, of course, is created this way.

ornithomancy: Gaining insight by watching the flight patterns of birds. Derived from the Greek *ornis*, for "bird," and *manteia* meaning

Introduction

"divination." You can add the suffix *-mancy* to the end of anything in Greek to mean prophecy by studying that object. For example, ichthyomancy (prophecy by looking at fish), daphnomancy (divination by studying leaves), chiromancy (palm reading), aleuromancy (divination with flour), cyclomancy (fortune-telling by staring at a spinning wheel), and lampadomancy (looking into flames). Basically, if it can be looked at, people have probably tried using it for divination. These techniques are also known as scrying.

reverie: A kind of **trance** caused by losing oneself in the rhythms of nature: snow falling, trees sighing in the wind, a flickering campfire, the rocking of ocean waves. The favorite pastime of poets.

synchronicity: Coincidence. There are two ways to look at coincidence: You can say it is merely a coincidence, so it means nothing. Or you can say there is no such thing as merely a coincidence; it must mean something. Synchronicity is coincidence that means something.

trance: Going into a state in which you are oblivious to your surroundings. Usually this involves becoming more focused on the internal world than on the external. Related to **reverie**. Often trance can be induced by repetitive activity—for example, the whirling dervish.

wombat: A short-legged marsupial native to Australia. Nocturnal, furry, and very cute. There aren't actually any wombats in this book, unfortunately. However, most people don't fully read the lexicon; they just glance at the words listed, right? I wanted to reward the few of you who studiously read all the way through these definitions, while those who didn't may read the whole book wondering, But when does the wombat appear?

1

Dropping the Spoon

A vague subterranean world reveals itself, little by little, and there the pale, grave, immobile figures that dwell in limbo loosen themselves from shadow and darkness. And thus, the tableau shapes itself, a new clarity illuminating and setting into play these bizarre apparitions; the world of spirits opens itself to us. —Gérard de Nerval, *Aurélia*

TECHNIQUE

Use common household dishes to peek through a window into altered consciousness.

TOOLS REQUIRED

1 comfortable chair, preferably of the cushy recliner variety
1 metal spoon
1 metal bowl or large ceramic plate
Notepad
Pencil

TIME REQUIRED

15 to 30 minutes, depending on how sleepy you are

RESULT

Experience the richness of hypnagogic imagery without forgetting it.

What is hypnagogia? You have experienced it countless times even if you don't know the name for it. You know the feeling. You're lying in bed or, even better, napping on the couch and the images of the day, the background thoughts that are always there, a constant hum, begin to take on a certain Cheshire cat leer; fanciful and odd images begin to swim by as effervescent as soap-bubble rainbows; fairy wings, a blue stag, patterns of red and blue (for me there is often a tunnel or kaleidoscope quality to the imagery) all swirl about, just as your consciousness relaxes its grip on reality.

You're experiencing hypnagogic imagery.

Hypnagogia in Greek means, roughly, abducting into sleep, or leading to sleep, depending on how you would translate it. It is that liminal in-between state where you are just beginning to dream but are still conscious.

The most famous example we have of hypnagogia fueling the creation of art is perhaps Samuel Taylor Coleridge's best-known poem, "Kubla Khan," which came to him after his reverie was broken by a knock on the door. Some might blame his visitor for interrupting the creation of the poem, but the truth is that without the knock on the door Coleridge would not have been cognizant enough to begin writing anything down or to remember it after.

Creative types, from writers to inventors and scientists, have long been aware of the rich trove of insight from our unconsciousness that can be made available to us through hypnagogic imagery. The list of inspired people who have made use of hypnagogic imagery is impressive: Beethoven reported obtaining ideas while napping in his carriage, Richard Wagner was inspired by hypnagogic imagery to write his Ring Cycle, Thomas Edison reported that during periods of "half-waking" his mind was flooded with creative images, and the philosopher John Dewey said creative ideas happen when "people are relaxed to the point of reverie."

Other geniuses knowledgeable of this technique include Carl Gauss, Sir Isaac Newton, Johannes Brahms, and Sir Walter Scott, but the person perhaps most successful at harnessing the creative energy was Salvador Dalí.

A well-read student of Sigmund Freud, Dalí—who never used drugs and drank alcohol (mostly champagne) only in moderation—turned to a most unusual way to access his subconscious. He knew that the hypnagogic state between wakefulness and sleep was possibly the most creative for a brain. Like Freud and his fellow surrealists, he considered dreams and imagination as central, rather than marginal, to human thought. Dalí searched for a way to stay in that creative state as long as possible, just as any one of us on a lazy Saturday morning might enjoy staying in bed in a semi-awake state while we use our imagination to its fullest. He devised a most interesting technique. Dalí would sit outside in the afternoon sun, drowsy after a large lunch, with a metal mixing bowl in his lap and a big spoon in his hand hovering over the bowl. As he began to drift off to sleep, his grip would relax and drop the spoon clanging into the bowl, waking him up. He'd then repeat the process, drifting along in this way, suspended between waking and dream, all the while taking in the hypnagogic imagery that would become the fuel for his paintings.

How simple, how obvious and elucidating this is! To think that those images of towering giraffes, lions stretching out of pomegranates, and four-dimensional tesseract crucified Christs were in fact straight out of dreams makes one realize that the mojo driving the king of surrealism (not to mention the likes of Newton and Beethoven) is in fact available to us right here and now, and the only cost is trading a nap for a drowsy state of temporary self-denial. The method also works for more than just wild imagery; Edison would do the same thing to gain inspiration for his inventions—drifting off to sleep in his rocking chair while holding a rock in his right hand, which would drop into a metal bucket on the floor.

My own experiments have shown that a ceramic plate works just as well as a metal bowl. Of course, some may prefer trying this experiment with a tape recorder instead of a pencil, but I have found operating "technologically advanced" equipment to be counterproductive toward fostering the desired dream state. Obviously if you are hunting for images rather than words, then only a pencil and paper will do. Another tip—you may want to dim the lights or even try writing with eyes closed. You will be surprised at how easy this is: You don't need to watch your hand to be able to scrawl somewhat legibly; your hand knows what it's doing!

So it is as simple as that. And best of all, there is absolutely no hangover or comedown to this trip. It is most pleasant, however, if you allow yourself the time to take a full and proper nap after you have gotten your notes and sketches down.

2

Intuition

The only real valuable thing is intuition.
—Albert Einstein

TECHNIQUE

Train yourself to get better at knowing what you already know (you just don't know it). Listening to your gut is a skill that grows stronger with practice, just like anything else. Trust me . . . actually, don't trust me—trust yourself!

TOOLS REQUIRED

A willingness to listen to your inner voice

TIME REQUIRED

This is less of something that you do for a given length of time and more of something you learn to always have available, at any given time.

RESULT

Finding your groove, getting a gut feeling, knowing when to trust your intuition.

Imagine an invisible structure, maybe a table or a chair made of the finest flawless glass or crystal, carefully designed so that it is quite invisible. Now imagine throwing a handful of fine sand onto this object: What was once impossible to see would be revealed. We can imagine in this hypothetical situation that the handful of beach sand we cast on the invisible surface would not reveal the object in complete detail; we would see only the outline of the thing where the sand clung to the object.

Or think of the way that dust, which is ever present in any house, is really noticeable only under certain circumstances of light, when a shaft of sunlight from outside comes through the windows at the right angle, especially when it is sunny outside but dim inside; then we can see a thousand dust motes dancing around, a small world usually invisible made seeable.

All of this admittedly awkward analogy is necessary because here I wish to talk briefly about the nature of magic, which is somewhat similar to the phenomena I just described, and since magic is an abstruse and odd concept, it seems that an abstruse and odd analogy might demonstrate it best. The tricks and rituals of magic allow us to perceive more clearly the invisible but palpable thing called instinct, intuition, gut feeling, or the unconscious. Magic is the casting of sand on that invisible object, simply making visible what was already there.

In other words, while we always have access to our intuition, to a sort of weak second sight or gut feeling—every ritual of divination, scrying, and so on brings into focus what, at some level, we are already aware of.

Let us examine one method here: tarot cards. While each specific card does have a sort of general meaning, how this is to be interpreted during a card consultation is open to a wide set of variables. Each card is a symbol rich with meaning that changes according to how the cards are dealt. Now it is not as though the user of a tarot deck supposes that there is some magical elf or genie guiding the cards into the proper spot to give the fortune-teller the proper meaning. No, the placement of the cards is completely random. If we allow no sentience or autonomy to the way the cards land, then the information derived from the cards is not inherent in the cards themselves but in the interpretation given to the random spread of symbols. The insight or prophecy is something within the seer/magus/fortune-teller that the ritual of divination provides access to.

With this in mind, we can say that no one way of accessing the insight/intuition is necessarily better or worse than another. The ritual of tarot and similar practices is merely a way to scatter a handful of dust, a dust made of ideas, upon the invisible structures that we already intuit. With this in mind, it seems that the most straightforward way to strengthen our skill at magic is by exercising our intuition.

The next time you are trying to figure something out, see what happens if you look at it less from the perspective of the rational mind and more from the perspective of your intuition. Trust your gut. The more you rely on your inner sense, the more you will be able to hear it.

3

Time Travel,

or

Neo-Ludditism

Men have become the tools of their tools. ·
—Henry David Thoreau

TECHNIQUE

Time travel by choosing a time period and using only objects that were available in that year. Think of it like a diet but giving up certain technology instead of food; try it for at least one day and see what happens.

TOOLS REQUIRED

Varies, depending on what year you pick. For example, if you say 1922, you can use a typewriter, a bicycle, an umbrella, and spaghetti. If you pick the year 1022, you can use a horse, an ax, fire, and all of nature for the day.

TIME REQUIRED

At least an afternoon or for the more advanced technique, one day a week.

RESULT

A different way of perceiving the objects that surround you. A realization that modern gadgets are maybe not as necessary as you thought. You will probably find that less truly is more and learn how possible it is to limit modern technology's influence.

Much of our modern culture is flashy and trashy. We all know it. I'm not going to waste your and my time by going into an extended monologue here about MP3 versus vinyl or cars versus bicycles, but believe me, I could. I'd rather skip right to looking for solutions.

Time Travel, or Neo-Ludditism

What does any of this have to do with the subject of this book? I believe that modes of low technology are more conducive to thinking in magical terms.

I agree that technology has brought us a lot. To anyone who says that the march of technology is a straight-out bad thing, I have to say I am a big fan of indoor plumbing. But we don't need to embrace the tide of the new simply because it is new. We must allow ourselves to choose the level and era of technology we wish to engage in. Otherwise, we risk losing ourselves in the onslaught of ever-proliferating technology.

I propose a middle path, whereby we learn to be discriminating about our usage of technology, to pick and choose which inventions benefit us. Let yourself decide what to take and what to use on an individual basis.

Some examples: The experience of reading by candlelight is different from reading by lamp. I'm not saying it's better, just different. *Vive la différence!* Travel by bicycle or walking is a richer mode of experience than being sealed off in a car. Why listen to recorded music at all when you could be playing an instrument and, better yet, playing a song with others?

Experiment with living in a different era of time for just a day. You might like how it feels so much that you make it a regular thing. I try to unplug as much as possible for one day each weekend; it is very relaxing to live in a slower era.

Try writing with a typewriter and it's a different experience. Non-microwaved food tastes better. Talking to a person in person feels better than Internet friends. The movies are in 3D, but so are the woods and the sea; videogames are now open-ended and multiplayer experiences, but so is reality. And it's way more hi-def. Also, it actually matters.

Here are some other experiments in time travel (aka neo-Ludditism) you should try:

Experiment 1
Fast from Facebook (or Twitter or whatever your thing is) for one week. Or even better, the whole Internet for a week. Unplug.

Experiment 2
Spend a day without your phone.

Experiment 3
Don't use anything invented after 1925 for twenty-four hours. (Then try it for forty-eight hours, or forty days, or . . .)

Experiment 4
Pick your favorite era, whether it's the 1960s or the 1860s, and use only the technology that would have been available then for a day. This includes all forms of media, transportation, styles of

dress, food, manners, customs, and the like. Experience the time of your choosing.

Experiment 5

Pick one day a week and unplug. Do this weekly. At first it might sound unbearable, but pretty soon, I promise you will find yourself looking forward to that one day each week!

4

The Life Line Walk

All that we love deeply becomes a part of us.
—Helen Keller

TECHNIQUE

Take a long walk; as you go remember as much as you can of your life story so far. Upon turning around to head home, imagine as much as you can of your life yet to come.

TOOLS REQUIRED

A pair of walking shoes and a mile or two of empty road at night.

TIME REQUIRED

At least an hour, maybe more, depending on how old you are.

RESULT

A clearer appreciation of time, a more lucid knowledge of your life story, and a better knowledge of what you want to do next.

They say that just before you die, your entire life flashes before your eyes, but why wait until then, when you're in such a hurry? I think you should take the time to let your life flash before you at least once a year—so you can experience it at your own pace. This spell is good for two things. It helps you see where you have been physically, emotionally, and spiritually, and I have found it's a great way to remind yourself of the things that really matter to you. Besides reminding you where you have been, it helps you see where you are going.

This big picture is something that we too often forget all about as we go through the day to day. Living life without ever thinking of where you are going and where you have been is like taking a long hike and missing all the scenery because you are too busy looking at your feet. For this exercise, go ahead and assume you

will live an average lifespan, so eighty-one years if you're female and seventy-six if you're a guy (sorry, dudes, them's the average breaks!). Walking is the part you actually have to *do* to experience; this won't work from an armchair.

To begin: Take a walk. I like to do this exercise on my birthday, but really any time of the year will work. You want plenty of time, at least an hour—I take a two-mile walk, but I'm in my late thirties, so it takes me that long. If you're a young grasshopper, you can probably do this in under a mile.

As you mosey along, divide up the length of the walk, block by block, into the different eras of your life. Estimate so you roughly know how much each block represents timewise. Depending on your age and how far you are walking, a block might equal one year or three or five years. As you pass each section that represents a period of your lifetime, take a while to remember as much as you can from that part of your life. Proceed chronologically. For the first few blocks let yourself recollect your childhood, remember your oldest memories: your parents the way they were back then, your playmates, old teachers, pets, hide-and-seek, whatever comes to mind. And with every few paces, let another month go by, and another memory. Continue in this way.

Obviously this experience will be different for everyone, depending on your age. Just spend a few minutes on each memory that comes to you; there is no time to dwell, life moves fast!

As you go, many old faces and memories, some that you haven't seen for a long time, will resurface. Most people will find that it is the highlights that will come back to them, their happiest moments, their greatest triumphs and heartbreaks. It can be a very emotional exercise. It allows you to look back on your life's path and see a picture that is more to scale, and truly representational, rather than just nostalgic remembering at random.

It is good to have a turnaround point in mind, some destination where you take a breath, grab a snack, a cup of tea, or whatever. Or better yet, it can be someplace in nature, or somewhere quiet in the city where you can pause and reflect. It's best if you do this outside and you have a view of the night sky. Nighttime is best because then there are fewer distractions while you walk. To walk at night is always to traverse within the self.

Now, take a moment to look up at the moon, the clouds, or clear night, see how many stars you can see, think to yourself, *These are the same stars I have walked beneath all my life.* Then look down at the earth, and say to yourself, *This is the same earth I have always walked on and will continue to walk upon.* This part of the spell is important because it helps connect your life walk to the greater whole so that it is more than mere navel-gazing.

When you're ready, begin walking home. Now, depending on your age, you might have to take the long way home to make the math work out. As you walk back, slowly project yourself into your future. For me every block represents about five years, and as I go I see myself getting older. Of course, I don't know exactly what will happen in the next half of my life, but I can imagine some of the likely things—hopes, dreams, possibilities.

This exercise is also a great way to think about major decisions in your life and the ramifications they are likely to have. Whether it is your career, your love life, or even a hobby or skill you are passionate about, as you walk, imagine the different possible outcomes and choices that may come up. Imagine some of the challenges and obstacles that you may overcome, and just as you did in the first half, you will be able to picture your whole future passing before your eyes. It is a trip.

When you get home, stop outside and look up at the stars one last time. If you have done the exercise right, you can imagine yourself to be somewhere in your eighties or nineties. (Of course, if you are actually already eighty, then you won't need to imagine. Instead, just continue to remember your life during the walk back, as you did in part one.)

Looking back over your life, ask yourself, What do you see? What are you proudest of? What are some of the things you are happy and content with, and what might be some things that from this perspective you would do differently? Now shake it off and, grateful for your time here, go inside; the rest of your life awaits.

5

Automatic Writing

Struggle to sketch the flow that already exists intact in mind.
—Jack Kerouac

TECHNIQUE

Write without thinking. Just go for it, with zero analysis of what you're scribbling.

TOOLS REQUIRED

Pencil, paper, and a loosey-goosey state of mind.

TIME REQUIRED

While you might not get this technique to work the first time, once you do, it takes only a few minutes to sink into and can be done for however long is comfortable for you.

RESULT

Ideas and sentences that are wild and wholly free from any sort of self-censorship. Brand-new territory.

Nineteenth-century mediums used automatic writing to attempt communication with the dead. It has also been suggested that Gertrude Stein used this method to produce her book *Tender Buttons*. It has been called the *ideomotor effect* by skeptics who claim it is nothing more than a subject making motions unconsciously. Exactly! It is funny that one school of thought attributes it to spirits and calls it one thing, another school of thought attributes it to the unconscious and calls it another, but neither really knows exactly what it is that they are talking about, whether they use the language of the spiritists or the scientists. It is easy enough to try for yourself.

Put a pencil in your hand, your hand to a piece of paper, and

write—write without thinking, whatever comes to your head, or better yet whatever comes to your hand, bypassing the head. It's a letting go. If it seems difficult, then just scribble loose scrawly lines for a while first.

Think of it as being less about the result and more about the process of learning how to loosen or tighten the valve of your attention as if it were a faucet.

The same loosening of critical thought and inhibition that facilitates automatic writing is the perfect antidote to writer's block. Often the biggest challenge for a writer facing a blank sheet of paper is the block created by one's own inner critic, and automatic writing is one way to push past that point, by not thinking about what you are writing at all, and instead just writing. Once the words start to flow and you feel ready to begin giving them more shape, go for it. This is also a useful technique for artists to play with by trying to doodle/draw subconsciously, without looking at the page. The results can be surprising and inspiring.

6

Establish a Creativity Ritual

*Before you can think outside of the box you have to start with
a box.* —Twyla Tharp

TECHNIQUE

Because we are creatures of habit, we can use the principle of ritual
to our advantage by triggering our creative mind. Create a ritual
that you can repeat anytime you are about to work on something
creatively.

TOOLS REQUIRED

The tools that you use to make your ritual can be as simple or as
complicated as you like.

Establish a Creativity Ritual

TIME REQUIRED

As often as you can. Every day, ideally. Repetition is the key. Day after day, for always. The more you repeat your ritual, the stronger the bond becomes between the ritual and the desired effect. Repetition is the key.

RESULT

A daily habit that will summon your creativity when you need it and will, over time, create a strong trigger that will focus the mind and summon the muse.

How can a creative person make sure that the muse will show up on time, day in and day out? It's an old problem that has been pondered to the point of cliché throughout the ages because there is no easy answer; there really is no guarantee that you can sit down to your work and be endlessly inspired. Sometimes we hit that wall. While there is no surefire way to make your muse show up on time, there is a trick that will make sure the muse arrives, if not punctually, then at least consistently. It's called having a ritual. Enacting a simple ritual every time you are about to create lets your subconscious know, "Hey, I'm working here, give me a hand."

Establish a Creativity Ritual

Most veteran artists are well aware of this practice (at least sub-consciously) and make use of a series of habits and superstitious tics every day before starting their work. Everybody does it differ-ently; the key is that whatever the ritual is, it is always repeated the exact same way.

Ritual is a way of using an action the body performs to prime the mind and emotions and creative energy into aligning where they need to be. If we examine ancient rituals such as the Eucha-rist, tribal war dances, and the Japanese tea ceremony, we find a similar process; the action precedes the desired inner state. The effectiveness of a priming ritual is well known to athletes too. NBA players often go through a long windup of tics before taking a free throw shot. One guy wraps the ball around his waist three times, another guy dribbles and then rubs his cheek. Jason Kidd blows a kiss before each free throw. Karl Malone would spin the ball on his fingers while whispering a secret mantra to himself. Put simply, the ritual calms the mind's jitters and lets the body know that you are beginning a series of moves that you have done many times before, so it can happen automatically. The ritual is the switch to go on automatic.

Great art is achieved much the same way—the artist becomes a conduit. Stravinsky, arguably the last great classical composer, would always play a couple of Bach fugues on the piano to warm up every day before he got down to the business of composing. Beethoven started each day with a cup of coffee; it had to be made out of exactly sixty coffee beans, so he would count them out before brewing the cup! (He would also sometimes pour pitchers of water on his hands while bellowing ideas for new songs, until his servant would crack up, and then Beethoven would get angry at him.)* One of my favorite living writers, Haruki Murakami, goes for a three- to four-mile run every morning before writing. Maya Angelou would check herself into a barren hotel room every morning, in order to write with no distractions. Film director David Lynch would go to the same Bob's Big Boy restaurant every day at 2:30 and drink a giant chocolate milkshake and a sugary coffee, for the rush of ideas he would get from all the sugar. John Cheever wrote in his underwear. William Faulkner worked at home in the library; since he didn't want to be disturbed and the door had no lock, he would remove the doorknob and take it with him!

This is my ritual. I like to write at a coffee shop, bringing with me just a notebook and pencils. This way I can't be distracted by the Internet or different chores that always need doing at home. Furthermore, I don't bring a book or anything. So I *have* to write— I would feel stupid sitting in a coffee shop and doing nothing at all, and I have my notebook with me, so it is the only choice I leave myself. As soon as I sip my first mouthful of coffee and spend a few

---

* For more great daily rituals of artists, I recommend the book *Daily Rituals* by Mason Currey.

minutes making sure that the two to three pencils I have brought with me are all nice and sharp, the ideas begin to flood into my head because I have trained my subconscious to recognize that "Hey—this ritual means it's idea-making time!"

WHAT'S YOUR PERSONAL RITUAL?

Design a simple priming ritual for yourself. Think of it as the on switch for your creativity.

Choose your ritual carefully, but don't be afraid of experimenting until you find the right one. It can be anything. You can create one on the spot. Try something you will be happy to do on a daily basis. Exercise is good, even just taking a daily walk, going for a run, playing a musical instrument, maybe a round of meditation, or even listening to a favorite record that you put on to get in the zone. Maybe you already have the beginnings of a ritual and you just haven't realized it, but now you can deepen it.

You can also steal a little bit from the greats. If there is one ritual common to a lot of big thinkers, it is drinking copious amounts of strong coffee! Tea works too and won't make you sleepy later. Your routine could be something as simple as sharpening three pencils or as odd as stripping down to write in the buff. *The important thing is the repetition.* Whatever it is, stick with it for at least two weeks, and do it every time before you sit down (or stand) to work on your art. Soon you will have made an agreement with your muse: "When I do this little ritual, it is time for us to roll up our sleeves and to get to work!"

Once you have habituated yourself to the simple routine of first the warm-up ritual and then the creative act itself (whether that is writing, music, or art), you will find that the opening ritual will summon the creativity you want, as easily as ringing a bell.

7

Ornithomancy

The future is no more uncertain than the present.
—Walt Whitman

TECHNIQUE

Divination with birds. Practice the art of letting flowing patterns inspire your thoughts. This basic technique is the backbone of all forms of divination.

TOOLS REQUIRED (PICK ONE)

A murder of crows
A flock of geese
A raft of coots
An exaltation of larks

A peep of chickens
A skein of geese
A colony of gulls
A charm of finches
A murmuration of starlings
A convocation of eagles
A paddling of ducks
A dissimulation of birds

TIME REQUIRED

This only takes a moment to try, but finding the right birds may take longer, depending on where you are.

RESULT

Unexpected insights, unusual creativity, whimsical ideas, fantastic notions, capricious inklings, eccentric hunches, and quixotic noumena.

Divination is one of the oldest forms of magic and has been around longer than civilization. It is the art of attempting to gain knowledge about what to do in the future by staring at something in the

present. Divination by examining the flight patterns of birds, also known as ornithomancy, or more commonly augury, is perhaps the oldest form of divination. It was particularly popular with the Romans and the Greeks. The verdict of the augur was consulted before any important decisions, from where to build a palace to when to go to war. As with any other form of divination (tea leaves, tarot cards, sticks, omens), by interpreting a random pattern, flashes of new insight are possible. While in theory any birds will do, I prefer divination by crows. It's easier than, say, wrens or chickadees. Crows just act like they have so much to say and they are trying so hard!

When you see a crow, let yourself notice any idea, feeling, or premonition that comes to your mind, however vague. One way to begin is by holding a question in your head while you watch the bird. It can be as simple as a yes or no question you have about the future. As you watch the crow, let it become the external thought that echoes in response to your internal thought and let this presentiment magnify and clarify gently. Practice, practice, practice.

FYI—ornithomancy is expressly forbidden by the Old Testament. Of course, so is eating pork chops, getting tattoos, and wearing "costly garments." Times change.

8

The Cloak of Invisibility

See everyone on the street before they see you, as a rule they won't see you. You feel a sort of invisibility.

—William S. Burroughs

TECHNIQUE

Use this trick from William Burroughs to pass undetected through crowded city streets. Learn how to direct your gaze at others to make yourself pass by unnoticed. Just by seeing people before they see you, you can make yourself pass unseen like a hobbit.

TOOLS REQUIRED

Your eyes. And a bit of practice. This one takes a little time to master, although some people do it naturally without realizing it. Works better the more people are around.

TIME REQUIRED

However long you want. (It does take a couple of tries to get the hang of it.)

RESULT

The ability to walk through a crowd unnoticed.

❦

I recently stumbled on this trick while listening to a William Burroughs lecture that he recorded for Naropa University.* Burroughs was a true American wizard, constantly pushing the envelope of the possible with his writing and thought. This technique of invis-

---

* Available for free online, these can be easily found by searching for Burroughs's Naropa lectures.

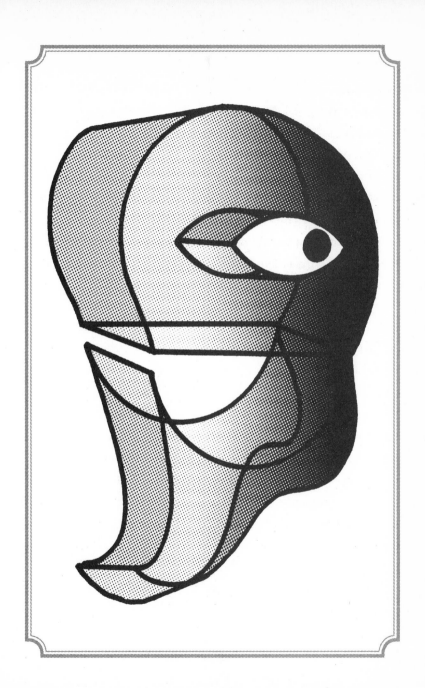

ibility is just one of many fascinating devices and spells he practiced; he is also well known for his investigations into synchronicity.

Burroughs claimed to have been taught the trick of how to walk unnoticed by others from "an old mafia don in Columbus, Ohio." The method works like this—when you are walking down the street, if you see someone walking toward you and you look at them first, then they are much less likely to look at you. That's it.

I know it doesn't sound like much on paper, but once you try it, it will begin to make sense. It is not that you become totally invisible, but you use this technique to reshape the perception of others. Whenever I have tried the technique and gotten into the groove with it, it is quite surprising how well it works. It is a bit like a game of chicken.

As you walk down the sidewalk, try to spot everybody walking toward you. Direct your gaze at everyone's eyes before their eyes have looked at you. Don't stare; that will make you more noticeable. Instead, practice a subtle gaze. The gaze is also different from one of just open friendliness and greeting, because again, that would make you more noticeable. It is neither friendly nor hostile, but is both firm and subtle. It is a look that has intent and is disinterested at the same time. As vague as that might sound, it's not that hard once you get it.

When you fix everyone you pass by with this special gaze, they will tend not to look directly at you. Most people are busy walking, talking, doing whatever anyhow—they aren't super aware of their surroundings, and *so they won't notice they aren't noticing you.*

The trick has its limitations; it's not going to make you able to pass by security cameras unregistered. But while you are in this mode, people you pass by will have a hard time remembering you afterward; since you were just on the periphery of their vision, you will be blurred. The more people there are on the street, the easier it is to do.

Burroughs doesn't go into why this trick works. He said that he was able to use it so well he became known as "el hombre invisible" and it helped him navigate the seedy and exotic sides of Tangiers and Mexico. I can only theorize as to how this works, but I think the explanation is actually pretty straightforward and less occult than it sounds. On a subconscious level, if a stranger is purposefully looking at our eyes, we are less likely to look directly at them. Call it social programming or call it biological. This is because there is a power dynamic at play. We can easily see this in many different animals, where a sustained gaze from a stranger can be perceived as a threat, as something to be avoided. I think the reason Burroughs's invisibility technique works has to do with subtle mechanics of human dynamics; this technique is just a way to play with one of the many invisible strings that have been there all along.

9

The Ganzfeld Technique,
or
the Poor Man's Sensory Deprivation Tank

You should look at certain walls stained with damp or at stones of uneven colour. If you have to invent some setting you will be able to see in these the likeness of divine landscapes . . . and then again you will see there battles and strange figures in violent action, expressions of faces and clothes and an infinity of things which you will be able to reduce to their complete and proper forms.

—Leonardo da Vinci, *Treatise on Painting*

The Ganzfeld Technique

TECHNIQUE

Use this old ESP method to zone out and see the movie playing in your head. Think of it as a way to tune your brain to a different station, sort of sensory deprivation for just your predominant senses. Not bad for a pair of silly-looking homemade goggles!

TOOLS REQUIRED

Ping-Pong balls
Scissors
Tape is helpful
Headphones and a loop of white noise

TIME REQUIRED

1 hour

RESULT

You can tune in to the background of your thoughts by blocking out surface noise and sight.

D.I.Y. Magic

As a child I spent many content hours studying the whorls and curlicues in the wood grain of my bedroom door. The arabesque patterns needed only the smallest prompting from my imagination to take on a life of their own and blossom into a fantastic bestiary of mercurial faces and creatures, dragons, imps, and gnomic animal heads, each knot of wood providing one eye. How easy it was to slip into the realm of pure imagination then!

Some might say this ability to see forms amid randomness is easily accessed only through the imagination of childhood, but I propose this skill is still available to one and all. As adults, however, we simply must approach the realm of the fantastic with a bit more intent. We must make the effort to clear away the clutter of the mundane.

One way to do this is through the Ganzfeld technique, one of easiest, quickest, and simplest methods for scrying (looking for insight by staring at something) that I have ever come across. I have appropriated this technique from its original usage in parapsychology. It comes to us from Gestalt psychologist Wolfgang Metzger's studies on the perception of a homogenous visual field, *Ganzfeld* being from the German for "entire field."

Although it was originally developed for use in Gestalt psychology in the 1930s and then used mainly in ESP research in the 1970s, its simplicity makes it a perfect pattern generator for practic-

ing the art of seeing something where there is nothing—animals in the clouds, a man on the moon, Jesus on a tortilla, and so on. This phenomenon is known as *pareidolia* and is often discussed as a sign of psychosis. Indeed many of the topics we shall discuss here are precisely that—a carefully modulated means of producing lucid madness. (In other words, depending on the fragility/rigidity of your own superego, proceed with these experiments at your own risk!)

Traditionally people scry by staring into crystal balls, which are hard to come by. Here is how to try it out with just a Ping-Pong ball. To begin, take two Ping-Pong balls and cut them in half; you will need two because they tend to have a small logo on one side, and you just want the blank half of the ball. Cut the ball in half with a razor or penknife; they cut easily along the seam. These will be placed over your eyes.

If you'd like, you can also fashion a way to hold the balls in place (tape, for example), although I have found that leaning back in a comfortable recliner or a field of grass works fine. Once you have the "goggles" ready, you need to seek out some headphones and white noise.

For white noise, you can use a radio tuned to a dead station, but be careful to avoid picking up bits of interference from other stations. I have come to rely on a free phone app, but you can use pretty much any white noise source—a fan in the background, a

passing rainstorm, or the like—the idea is simply to block out the usual sonic distractions.

You now have all the elements for a fully portable and efficient miniature sensory deprivation kit!

Turn on the white noise, try on your goggles, then kick back and let your subconscious get rolling. Be patient, because nothing usually happens for the first fifteen minutes or so. However, soon a flowing series of imagery will coalesce out of the static. Your brain is *expecting* to hear and see stuff because you are still taking in noise and the visual stimuli of a light source. Eventually your brain will begin creating images to make up for the lack of stimuli.

Note that in the original experiments exploring the Ganzfeld technique, a red light was set up in front of the person doing the experiment. I have not found this necessary, but a rear bike light makes for a great ad hoc red light source if you want to try that.

I believe the Ganzfeld technique to be one of the most elementary/introductory means for scrying. Later on we will address more advanced methods—but for now take some time to familiarize yourself with the feeling of turning off the ego and seeing what the rest of your brain is up to. Be receptive to the images that float to the surface, mold them gently; they are like downy feathers on the surface of a pond, and the slightest disturbance will send them reeling. I recommend that for this exercise you don't worry about trying to verbalize anything, but *do* keep a pencil and sketch pad handy to capture any interesting imagery you experience.

In case I still haven't convinced you to give this a serious whirl, here is a teaser: The myriad riches available by staring at our own brains, as it were, are reminiscent of the epiphany Flaubert ascribes to his hero in *The Temptation of Saint Anthony.* At the end of this book, the saint, peering into an ocean tide pool, experiences a rush of pareidolia stimulated by the brack and flotsam of the cradle of life itself:

> *A phosphorescence gleams around the whiskers of seals and the scales of fish. Urchins revolve like wheels, horns of Ammon uncoil like cables, oysters set their hinges creaking. . . .*
>
> *Vegetable and animal can now no longer be distinguished. Polyparies looking like sycamores have arms on their boughs. Anthony thinks he sees a caterpillar between two leaves; but a butterfly takes off. He is about to step on a pebble; a grey grasshopper leaps up. Insects resembling rose-petals adorn a bush; the remains of may-flies form a snowy layer on the ground.*
>
> *And then the plants become confused with the rocks.*
>
> *Stones are similar to brains, stalactites to nipples, iron flowers to tapestries ornate with figures.*
>
> *In fragments of ice he perceives efflorescences, imprints of shrubs and shells—so that he hardly knows whether these are the*

imprints of the things, or the things themselves. Diamonds gleam like eyes, minerals pulsate.

And he no longer feels any fear!

He lies flat on his stomach, leaning on both elbows; and holding his breath, he watches.*

---

* From Gustave Flaubert, *The Temptation of Saint Anthony*, translated by Kitty Mrosovsky (New York: Penguin, 1980).

10

Yoga

Yoga is called balance.
—Bhagavad Gita

TECHNIQUE

Calm and ground your mind and mood by moving your body. Sure, it's healthy for you, but we are also just beginning to understand how yoga can be calming, and meaningful, on much more than just a physical level.

TOOLS REQUIRED

Yourself. Nothing else. That's it. You don't even need a mat or fancy, tight shorts to get started. But a mat is nice to have. Also, if you're a beginner, it's good to take a class or two, but once you know a few moves you can do it on your own.

TIME REQUIRED

I recommend starting with just 5 to 10 minutes a day.

RESULT

Greater mental and physical balance, which is needed for all the other spells, techniques, and recipes in this book!

⁂

Unlike many ideas in this book, the way to try this one out for yourself is already well known. In fact, it is so popular, I may have to convince you that it should be classified as magic in the first place!

Few ancient ideas have grown in popularity as swiftly in Western culture in the past fifty years as yoga. While it was introduced to the West as early as the 1890s, it really did not become popular until the 1960s. Within our culture, yoga is still a relatively young phenomenon, and it's interesting to imagine what this ancient technique may evolve into as it is adapted by Western civilization and what far-reaching effects yoga will have on us as a culture.

D.I.Y. Magic

I expect many people may sneer at this book for its clumsy fumbling at the buttons of the sublime. I also expect that the same folks who believe the do-it-yourself philosophy for approaching magic is too lowbrow will be those people who think that a topic like yoga has no place in this book, that it has become too commonplace and too well known to be worthy of inclusion in a collection about the esoteric. I disagree. The mage seeks out the truth, that which *works*, in the high and the low, in the commonplace and the obscure, with equal diligence.

Despite its growing ubiquity, yoga remains one of the oldest and most powerful systems of magic—integrated mental/physical/spiritual discipline—ever realized by humankind. The number of yoga practitioners has tripled to eighteen million in this country in the last decade. I think that many of us are comfortable with it because it can be viewed as a physical exercise, yet also fulfills a craving for spiritual development that was once met largely by Christianity in the West. Yoga appears conveniently secular, with none of the baggage that is a part of Christianity's cultural legacy. Scholars theorize that yoga has its roots in shamanism and ritual magic. This taproot of archaic shamanism is shared by many other traditional Eastern practices such as qigong and tai chi.

Yoga is a quick and easy way to relax at home, at work, or wherever you happen to be, at any time of day. The following are some simple yoga applications and sequences that are short and effective and can be done in five to ten minutes each.

Downward Dog

If you were on a desert island and could take only one yoga pose, it would probably be this. It is easy, refreshing, and basic. Sort of like a toe touch, except your hands are farther out in front of you so that your body makes an upside down *V.* This pose stretches the calves and hamstrings, builds strength in the arms, and gives your brain an invigorating rush of blood. A beautiful way to wake up. Try pedaling out your legs a few times before moving on to the next pose.

Cobra

The perfect balance to downward dog is cobra; it is sort of like a downward dog reversed. Sweep forward from downward dog so that your pelvis sinks to the ground while your arms remain straight and your chin and chest lift upward—this creates an energizing arc to the back.

Upward Salute

Finish this series off by doing the simplest of stretches. With feet squarely planted, raise high both arms to the sky and gently arch your back. This pose is so natural a lot of people do this upon first waking already, without even thinking of it as yoga. With this simple sequence you will be starting your day with a clear head and bright energy.

D.I.Y. Magic

As you try some of these simple postures, you will find that the connection between the body and the mind is a powerful one. Yoga does not have to happen solely in a yoga studio but can be an integral part of your daily life, as helpful, habitual, and quick as brushing your teeth. It requires no special tools, can be practiced by anyone anywhere, and can be used to help you achieve the particular result you desire right now—whether that be to relax or to revitalize and refresh.

11

Bibliomancy

He opened the book at random, or so he believed, but a book is like a sandy path which keeps the indent of footsteps.

—Graham Greene

TECHNIQUE

One of the oldest tricks in the book, literally. Use the principles of chaos to flash insight into any question. Here's how: Think of a question, pick a book, flip to a random passage, and apply the first thing you read to answer your question.

TOOLS REQUIRED

Any book works—but some are more "magical" than others. Just like some people give better advice than others. Here are a few books that work well:

> The Bible
> *The Collected Works of William Shakespeare*
> *The Teachings of Don Juan*
> The Upanishads
> *The Cantos* by Ezra Pound
> This book
> *Moby-Dick*
> *The Catcher in the Rye*
> Your favorite book

TIME REQUIRED

5 minutes

RESULT

Surprisingly (sometimes shockingly) pertinent advice! Also, you can say, "No, I haven't read *Moby-Dick*, but I have done bibliomancy with it."

Bibliomancy

First of all, what is a book? It is a form of mental telepathy. As the writer of this book, my thoughts are conveyed to you, my dear reader, with greater precision, grace, and care than I could manage if you and I were to have a conversation. Books are the mind of the author preserved in the amber of ink. Lucky for us that when someone gets a good idea it is often written down; when we read Shakespeare, Virginia Woolf, J. K. Rowling, and Plato, we are experiencing the thoughts and imagination of that author at their most concentrated and refined. People ask, If you could dine with any great author from the past that you admire—such as Kafka, Proust, or Dickinson—who would it be? Such a silly question! Because of course you *can* have lunch with Thoreau or Stephen King, or whomever you want, and today, if you choose. In the same day you can hang out with Jane Austen all afternoon and then spend the evening with Mark Twain. We turn to books for the same reason we enjoy conversations with other people—for fun, for humor, for comfort, for companionship, and for advice.

We do not always have to spend the whole day with a friend. Sometimes just a quick phone call is plenty; in the same way, one does not have to reread *The Brothers Karamazov* or *The Hobbit*, or whatever your favorite book is, every time you want to experience that author's ideas. You can dip into it quickly; that is what this exercise is about. Furthermore, this spell demonstrates a novel way to get advice from your favorite authors. Just as we turn to our friends for conversation, for advice or comfort or inspiration, we can turn to books for the same thing.

Here is how: Take the book of your choice and place it in front of you lying on its spine. Now hold a question in your mind; it could be about anything: What should I do about this situation? What is the next step for me? It could be a more abstract question, a why-type question. Anything works. Now that you have the question in mind and the book of your choosing in hand, you are ready to begin. You can let the book fall open at random; that's the traditional method. Or you can rifle the pages back and forth a few times between your thumb and index finger, like a deck of cards. Do all of this without looking at the book; you are not choosing a passage, you are letting the passage choose you. You can close your eyes. Whenever you are ready, stop, point to a line with your finger, and see where you have landed. Read the passage out loud.

Now look for ways to apply that sentence to the question in your mind. You will often be surprised at how spot-on the answer is. It can feel quite uncanny. This can be a very easy way to gain new perspective into whatever is troubling or perplexing you. It is often the same way in conversations with friends; often insight is gained less from specific advice that a person gives us than from some oblique chance comment.

Once you try bibliomancy, the next question becomes, Why does this work so well? The answer, I think, has to do with the

quality of the book and the property of truth. When something like a great book has wisdom in it, it transcends the place and time it was written in, the city and culture and language it was written in. It becomes a truth for all humanity. Of course you can use just about any book, as long as it is one that holds truth. The world is full of portents and signs if we would learn how to see them.

12

Manifestation

With our thoughts we make the world.
—Buddha

TECHNIQUE

Like attracts like. Pay attention to what you expect from your day, your life, your world. If you want to do something, the first step is to imagine yourself doing it.

TOOLS REQUIRED

Optimism

Positivity

An awareness of the ideas in your head that you project upon
    reality

D. I. Y. Magic

TIME REQUIRED

While it takes only a moment to use, it must be cultivated day by day.

RESULT

Find whatever you're looking for just by expecting to find it. You won't see it unless you think it's there. The applications are limitless, and the possibilities are only limited by your own imagination.

A friend of mine is a genius at finding free stuff. He has a huge collection of just about everything: dozens of bicycles, music gear, several espresso machines, a big shoe collection, sports gear, and so on, and he found it all for free. Whenever we are driving somewhere together, he spots a free pile that I haven't noticed. And he usually finds something worthwhile when we pull over. It's not that he is lucky so much as that he is looking. (Also, just last week I gave him a surfboard that was gathering cobwebs in my backyard, because I knew that he would want it. And the very evening I wrote this paragraph, my friend stopped by and claimed to have found a free box with a very nice classical guitar and a working flamethrower!)

Like attracts like. Ever notice you say the name of a person you haven't thought of in ages and then you bump into her later that day? It's weird, right? I'm not saying that one causes the other. I'm just observing.

We find what we expect to find. This is a basic human principle. The magus is one who uses that principle as a fulcrum. By changing what we expect to find, we see that it was there all along. What would you like to see happen, and what is the mind state that is most conducive to that possibility?

Enter that mind state, go about your business, and see what happens. We must sidle up to reality gently, treating it as a friendly but skittish kitten. You can't force reality to match up to your wishes. But if you are looking, you are more likely to find what you are looking for. This is one of the most underused truths—we see what we expect to see; by cultivating this principle we can manifest powerful discoveries, and find whatever we are looking for. It's a sleight of mind rather than a sleight of hand. The mark whom you are trying to con is yourself. Or your reality. Or your perception of reality. What was the difference to begin with?

13

Build Your Own Tarot Deck

The diverse opinions of eminent authorities on the Tarot symbolism are quite irreconcilable.

—Manly P. Hopkins

TECHNIQUE

Build your very own tarot deck from the ground up. You can choose symbols and themes that are already meaningful to you. Now you don't have to read some book about what the cards "mean." You made them, you tell me!

TOOLS REQUIRED

Blank index cards (use the plain side) or nice card stock cut to size
Pens, pencils
(Also, this one is a lot of fun to do with a group of friends.)

TIME REQUIRED

While it may take a few hours to make your own deck, once you begin to do readings you will become fluent so you can take as long or be as quick as you like.

RESULT

A new understanding of the age-old symbol generator that is the tarot, as well as your own pack of cards.

I came to tarot as a skeptic. I needed a job in college and answered an ad in the paper for a telephone psychic. Frankly, I thought it would be only a small matter of time before I was discovered and fired for being an imposter who didn't really have psychic powers. But what the heck, I figured I would try it out for a week and collect at least one paycheck. Since I didn't know how to be psychic, I

checked out a book from the library on tarot cards. I photocopied the tarot cards from the library book and pasted them onto the front of a deck of regular playing cards.

This worked surprisingly well. For the first dozen calls that I got, I kept a book on how to read tarot open on my desk. As calls came in, I would lay out the cards for the caller and be furiously flipping through the book to look up the meanings of the cards while I told people their fortunes. "You got the five of swords, that means . . . uh . . . hang on!" To my amazement, it worked. My customers were happy. Not only did they get good advice, to my surprise again and again the use of the cards provided insight into their problems and needs that I would not have been able to offer otherwise. The use of the cards as a focal point allowed people to readily open up more about their own desires and fears than they would have if they were just talking to a person without the cards. Without any innate psychic powers of my own, without any trickery or subterfuge, I was successful as a telephone psychic.

Gradually I came to learn what the symbols on the cards stood for, and my readings became faster. The cards seemed to "get lucky" time and time again. I couldn't believe it! I gave people counsel on everything from the future to the past, on family drama and romance and work and personal stuff. It worked without me needing any special powers beyond listening and empathy. Anyone can do it; you don't need special powers.

Build Your Own Tarot Deck

This was a huge revelation to me. I have since realized the tarot deck works because it is filled with ancient archetypal symbols. That they are archetypal simply means they represent basic fears, hopes, dreams, challenges, and desires that are present in everybody's life. When you begin talking about the symbols that you see in the cards, the person whose fortune you are reading gets a shock of recognition.

While to this day I have a great deal of respect for the traditional tarot cards, I insist there is nothing mysterious about how they work, and the same powerful insights and empathetic revelations can occur using a deck of cards with your own homemade symbols. While the traditional tarot deck is very well balanced and chock-full of powerful archetypal symbols, there is nothing inherently supernatural going on, and for this reason I think that making your own deck can give you a better understanding of not only how archetypes and symbols work but also how card readings work, and even how the traditional tarot works. For the traditional tarot deck is but one book, yet an infinity of books wait to be written.

I was inspired to create my own tarot deck by looking at the images from a Mexican *tablas de lotería* board hanging on my kitchen wall (brightly colored pictures on individual squares of *la luna, la mano, el borracho, el corazón*; fifty-four in all). I realized they could be just as useful in telling a person's fortune as the tarot, if

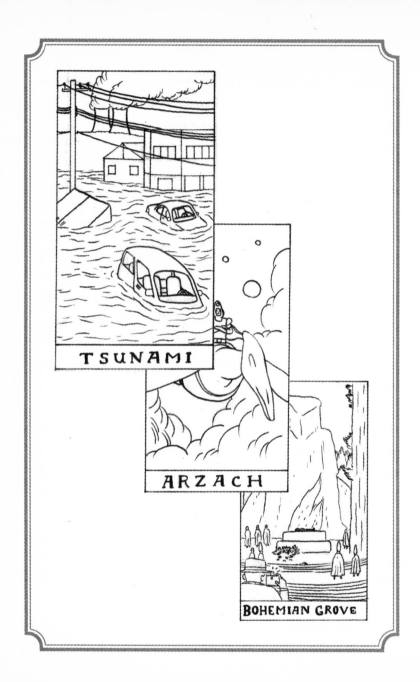

TSUNAMI

ARZACH

BOHEMIAN GROVE

not more so, because they are not cramped by the accumulation of centuries of interpretations. I started experimenting with these images, and pretty soon I was making up my own. Sadly, I can't draw worth a hill of beans (in fact, I can't even draw a hill of beans), but even stick figures and sloppy sketches will get the job done. If you can actually draw, then it's even more fun. I have workshopped this idea with comic book artists, and they have come up with really amazing and beautiful cards.

With a little experimentation, it is simple to construct a full deck using whatever symbols you want, a deck that you, the practitioner, can modify to suit your own preferences and tastes. The personalized deck should have that much more potency. It can be tweaked and tailor made; it doesn't come out of a box but from the deck maker's thoughts; each will be as unique as the individuals who made them.

To begin, make your own list of cards. Fifty-four is a good number to shoot for, even though technically a proper tarot deck has seventy-eight cards. You can start out with fewer. You can calibrate a deck of cards from scratch that will suit you individually as a fortune-teller, or you can use this short list of basic archetypes to get you started. Feel free to use any of these that you like; it is also of course fine to steal ideas from the original tarot deck or the *tablas de lotería.* There ain't no hard-and-fast rules. You just want cards that are archetypal.

Some Ideas

The Dreamer

The Alligator

The Crow

Florida

The Hammock

The Sea

The Dancer

Jesus

New Jersey

The Pulled-Pork Sandwich

Walt Disney

The Earthquake

Mercy

Beer

The Knife

The Mermaid

The Businessman

The Guitar Player or Troubadour

The Gangster

The Corrupt Politician

The Polar Bear

The Ghost

Mr. Whiskers

The Falcon

The Beast
The Bicycle

Once you've decided what to include, it's time for the pack of blank index cards. (Regular blank white paper works just as well too. You just have to do more work with the scissors.) On each card, draw one image from your list. The picture can be as simple or complex as you want; generally more detail is more helpful. Glue the images to a deck of regular playing cards. This makes them easier to shuffle.

Now you're ready to tell somebody's fortune. It's best to practice on yourself a few times before moving on to friends and eventually the biggest challenge—strangers (this is known as doing a cold reading).

Here is a simple layout and some tips to get you started. The easiest layout is known as the simple Celtic cross. You place one card in the middle, and then one card above it, one below it, and one each to the left and the right of your center card, five cards in all. You can place them facedown and explain what the positions signify before flipping them over. The center card represents the present. The card to the left, the past, and the card to the right, the future. The lower card represents that which is hidden; the higher card signifies outward influences. There are dozens of other traditional ways to do the layout, some of them quite complicated. I recommend checking out a book or two from the library if you

want to go deeper with studying the tarot. This is one case where it is better to skim a handful of books on the subject, rather than read deeply from just one, because they will all offer slightly different interpretations, and it is best to grasp the ideas behind the symbols from multiple vantage points. Like cooking or playing guitar, once you are familiar with the basics you should feel free to improvise.

How you actually interpret the cards takes practice. They are symbols. Pretend you are a Jungian analyst parsing the content of a dream. Read into everything. Think out loud as you go and ask questions of your audience to see if you're on the right track. The skeptic will see this as cheating because the skeptic is a knucklehead, too obtuse to separate the concrete from the abstract. People like this are boors and best avoided altogether.

Magic works via power of imagination. Imagination works by metaphor. Let us say you have dealt a card with a picture of a bird drawn on it. What does that image bring to mind in the context of the other cards that have been dealt, and in the context of its position in the spread, and in the context of the person whose fortune you are reading? For example, a bird brings to mind flight, perhaps a symbol of freedom or rising above a situation, but in conjunction with a card depicting the ocean, it might connote travel overseas. It is important to understand that a tarot reading is a collaboration between the fortune-teller and the subject. It should not be a guessing game. If you are having trouble reading the cards, the solution is to simply ask your subject for help. Just ask, What were you doing yesterday? What were you doing last week? What has been on your mind lately? How do you feel about the question you asked? It is very helpful to ask basic questions like these; once you know the history of your subject, all of the symbols on the cards will fall into place.

Interpreting tarot symbols, whether the traditional or home-made, is very similar to interpreting dreams. If the meaning laid out in the symbols is not immediately clear, it is simply because more information is needed. A dream, or a tarot reading, becomes clear if the details are filled in. All these things should come into play, but ultimately it is about a feeling, not a set of rules. If used properly, the cards will allow you to tap into powerful intuitions that you would not have been aware of otherwise.

14

The Coin Trick

In some sense man is a microcosm of the universe; therefore what man is, is a clue to the universe. We are enfolded in the universe. —David Bohm

TECHNIQUE

Use a quarter to tap into your intuition and find out what you really want when you're faced with a choice. Call heads or tails, flip the coin, catch it; but then, just before you look at it, ask yourself if you're hoping for heads or tails. Don't bother to check the quarter; it just goes right back in your pocket.

D. I. Y. Magic

TOOLS REQUIRED

A decision you're unsure about
A quarter

TIME REQUIRED

A split second

RESULT

A decision has been snatched from thin air.

What is a choice? What difference does it make whether we choose something with free will or just allow chance to dictate our choice? Quantum physics gives us some insight into these fifty-fifty decisions. If you don't look at a quarter after you have flipped it, was it ever really heads or tails? Consider the Heisenberg uncertainty principle: The more precisely we observe the position of a particle, the less precisely its momentum can be known. In other words, science has shown that *the act of observing changes the thing being observed.* Or take Schrödinger's cat, a thought experiment that states that

when something has a truly random chance of being one way or the other, technically *it is both at the same time,* until we observe the outcome. It is almost as though the flipped quarter in your pocket never truly stopped spinning. And then there are the physicists who believe that every time we make a choice, we are creating a universe: one where that is the choice made! This is called the many-worlds interpretation of quantum mechanics, and I know that it sounds totally nuts, but this is seriously believed by people (58 percent of quantum physicists) who do a whole lot more math than I would ever want to do.

So if you were already having a hard time making up your mind about choosing A or B, just imagine that choice will create two entirely separate universes, two distinct realities! Sorry, that won't make the decision easier . . . but it does make it more exciting, no? What are you, other than the sum of every decision you have ever made up until this point? What is history, other than the sum of every choice every human has ever chosen?

I bring up the idea of the many-worlds theory because it underlines the importance of human choice. We create the world we inhabit with every decision we make. This fact is the central tenet of existentialism, and to fully grasp the profundity of it gives incredible weight to our choices. It can also be paralyzing. The coin trick is a simple bit of sleight of hand: an exercise in flippancy, by saying, Let fate decide, but then snatching the reins back from fate at the last second and asking, What did I want the coin to land on, heads or tails?

The magus is one who balances on this paradox: both recognizing the incredible freedom in choice and yet not becoming overwhelmed by the limitless possibilities inherent in any decision. At any moment you are free to go anywhere, choose anything, do or be whatever you please. Every choice is paradoxically both as gigantic and powerful as choosing a whole universe from the infinite possibilities the future could become, and as simple and easy as a coin toss. Heads or tails?

15

Schizophrenia as Oracle

There is no great soul without a touch of madness.
—Seneca the Younger

TECHNIQUE

Reconsider how you interact with insanity—in many older cultures
the madman was respected as a seer and an integral part of society.
You probably come across people who see reality in a very different
way from anyone else, somewhere in your community. Talk to
them and see if you can learn anything.

TOOLS REQUIRED

The main thing is to break down your own prejudices and societal
conditioning about insanity. It is easy to write a person off because

he or she has mental health problems. The tools needed here are a mind-set of compassion and openness.

TIME REQUIRED

Depends on how long you are comfortable outside of your comfort zone.

RESULT

Maybe just an interesting and unusual interaction with a fellow human being. Probably some insight into a worldview that's very different from your own. Maybe even a new friend.

When I was a young man and often in need of guidance and counsel, I found that the best advice and insight available was often surprisingly from a crazy lady who lived out of a shopping cart in front of the library. Her favorite topics of conversation revolved around a magical book that controlled the weather and was also tied into global politics and conspiracy theories. She also listened to what I had to say; it's just that her answers came from a place, a worldview so drastically different from mine that it never failed to provide a radically fresh perspective that I hadn't thought of.

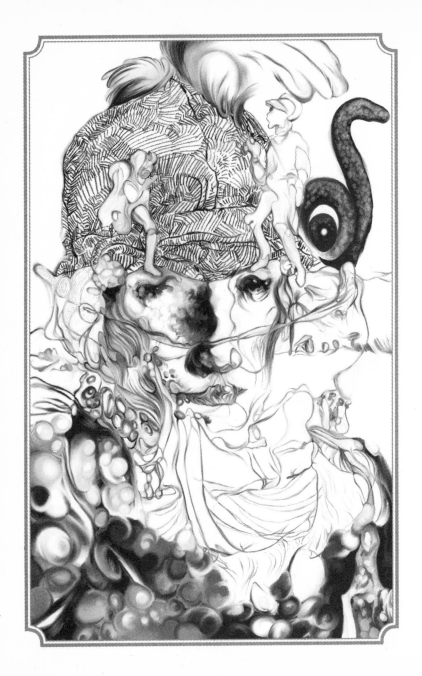

Later on I worked as a social worker with many schizophrenic clients. I have also known a few close friends who have lost their minds, and I am not suggesting that schizophrenia is not a terrible and debilitating disease. I am suggesting that our society, by stigmatizing it, castigating it, and casting it out of our rational framework, has made it a worse condition to suffer than it is in some cultures, where the madman is seen to hold a kind of wisdom. While working in mental health, I learned that for meaningful dialogue to occur between the sane and insane, it is often the sane people who must change their rigid mode of conversation. Most people are too afraid to hear anything more than nonsense. As is often the case, just beyond prejudice, wisdom can be found. Here are three things you can do to open up and experience this. They may require that you stretch yourself out of your comfort zone, but I encourage you to do just that.

Volunteer

There are countless volunteer opportunities, at shelters, soup kitchens, and outreach programs. These are going to be associated with different organizations depending on where you are, but every city has dozens, and they are usually happy to take on volunteers. My experience has been that there is a lot of overlap between services meant to help the mentally ill and the impoverished and people struggling with addiction. Spend some time helping out in your local soup kitchen or shelter and you will expand your experience of humanity sevenfold.

Talk to People

Next time someone asks for change, don't just hand him or her a quarter and keep walking; chat with them for a while. Our society stigmatizes poverty as much as insanity. From the simple act of chatting, not only will you likely be appreciated but you are probably going to learn something, which happens whenever you step outside of your normal range of social interaction.

Be Open

Don't flee from "crazy talk." You see it so many times, especially in crowded cities, a person talking to hallucinations or voices, while a crowd splits around the person as if they were not even there, as if that person were a ghost. Of course you should use common sense; don't approach someone who seems agitated or possibly dangerous in any way. But my experience has often been that the mentally ill folks I have struck up a conversation with have also been some of the gentlest, kindest souls I have met, and they have more to share than most because they have seen so much that is unique and different.

16

Lucid Dreaming

Buddha Shakyamuni often told his disciples to regard all phenomena as dreams. . . . Dreams represent just one type of illusion. The whole universe arises and dissolves like a mirage. Everything about us, even the most enlightened qualities, are also dreamlike . . . so in going to sleep, you're just passing from one dream state to another.

— Palden Sherab Rinpoche

TECHNIQUE

The first step is to remember your dreams: Keep a dream journal. The second step is to recognize when you are dreaming. There's a variety of ways to check; you can see if you are able to float in the air, that's usually a sign. You can read something—text doesn't stay put in dreams. You start by doing this reality check in reality, until by force of habit you check while you're dreaming and become aware that it's a dream. The third step is to do anything you can dream of.

TOOLS REQUIRED

The primary ingredient is good recall of your dreams. This makes you more aware of them, and for that you need a dream journal and a pencil by your bed.

TIME REQUIRED

This actually takes no extra time at all because you sleep and dream every night already.

RESULT

Seriously unlimited! You can fly, for starters; you can meet anyone, go anywhere, and do anything. Realizing the freedom of lucid dreaming is a step toward realizing that your potential in waking life is also as limitless as your imagination.

Lucid Dreaming

Lucid dreaming is the art of realizing you are dreaming while you are dreaming. Once you realize you're dreaming, you can do anything you want within the dream.

Many people think that once you realize you are in a dream you will wake up. That's not true. Instead, you realize the world you are in is a projection of your own mind, and then the possibilities of that reality become unlimited.

The first step to doing this is simply to be able to consistently remember your dreams. This is often harder than it should be because we wake up with an alarm blaring and it's time to go. Try to give yourself a few moments each morning before you begin the day to lie in bed and recount where you just were in dreamland. Often it takes a while for anything to surface, but once a single image tugs on the line of memory, you can quickly haul up the whole fish from the depths.

It is also very helpful to keep a dream journal. Throughout history, in many cultures, dreams were treated as an important part of life. In some cultures, the time spent dreaming is seen as just as important as waking life and sometimes even more meaningful. Keeping a dream journal for a week or two drastically improves dream retention because the act of transcribing your dreams teaches your brain that you expect to remember your dreams. It also shows your subconscious that you are taking it seriously, and when you do that the subconscious often will oblige. Like a long-neglected student who feels he has finally been given a

chance to shine, the subconscious will put on its best performance after a period of neglect.

Once you can remember your dreams fairly consistently, you are ready to proceed to the actual work of lucid dreaming. There are several methods for encouraging lucid dreaming. The first thing to try is to get into the habit of performing a reality check. Throughout the day you must pause and ask the question, Am I dreaming? Getting into the habit of entertaining this thought while awake means that eventually you will ask the question while you are asleep. Your consciousness follows the same patterns asleep as it does awake.

When you do a reality check, you will need some way to know whether the reality you inhabit is a dream or not; there are certain telltale signs. One method is to periodically look at your hands. If they seem stable, and aren't metamorphosing into other forms, then you're not dreaming. To be habituated enough to check this while you are asleep, you need to run the check every few hours while awake. Another trick is to flick a light switch on and off or to read a book in the dream (often printed text can't maintain integrity within dreams). On the surface these ideas sound silly. But the idea is to train yourself to have a frame of reference that is stable and habitually checked. Really, I think that just asking yourself if you're dreaming is often strong enough to alert you to the dream.

Here are a few more tricks practiced by knowledgeable oneiro-nauts (explorers who navigate the dream world):

- Have a mantra that you chant before bed—for example, "I will remember my dreams tonight. I will realize that I am dreaming."

- If you wake in the middle of the night, jot a few words down on a piece of paper. This will improve recall the next morning. This helps with lucid dreaming simply by making you more aware of your dreams; it exercises your basic dream awareness.

- Vivid dreams are easier to remember. Good sleep produces vivid dreams. Sleep well.

- Some people are able to choose what they are going to dream about by thinking about it as they are falling asleep. With this in mind, you can think about meeting someone in the dream who will tell you, "You are dreaming." Or dreaming of a scene or a sign that will help you realize you are dreaming.

Personally, I think one of the easiest ways to get into lucid dreaming is to take naps. I don't know why, but they come easier in the day.

Learning how to manipulate the reality of your dreams is a great training ground for the practicing magician because the same malleability of reality can be found in waking life by those

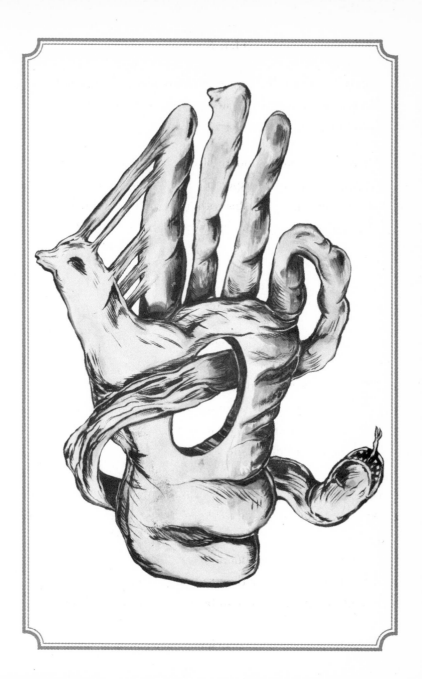

who know. I had a lucid dream this morning, in fact, and when I woke up I felt the day held more opportunity and potential than I had seen the day before. Just as dreams echo life, life can echo back what we learn in dreams. This is similar to the thinking behind Tibetan dream yoga, a practice dating back many centuries. As the adept is able to realize that a dream is only a world created by the self, an illusion (*maya*), he or she will also come to see how the world itself is a vast illusion.

17

Surfing Waves of Synchronicity & the Interpretation of Random Events

There is no such thing as chance; and what seems to us mere accident springs from the deepest source of destiny.
—Friedrich Schiller

TECHNIQUE

Learn how to interpret your synchronicity and luck to your advantage. Find your groove.

D.I.Y. Magic

TOOLS REQUIRED

Awareness
(It can be helpful to keep a small synchronicity notebook and
  watch the improbable pile up.)

TIME REQUIRED

A few minutes

RESULT

A better awareness of the people, things, ideas, and places that are
in the same groove as you are.

❦

I once dated a girl who was freaked out by digital clocks because
whenever she glanced at one, the numbers read 1:11 or 2:22, and
so on. She took this to be a very ominous and spooky portent for
some reason. Of course there was no particular reason to see these
coincidences as ominous or bad; she could just as easily have as-
sumed this random sign was lucky or auspicious.

Often we find exactly what we are looking for in the daily

coincidences we bump up against. Synchronicity is the coincidence that begs to be noticed. The art of synchronicity surfing, or finding your luck, is related to the manifestation technique we looked at a few chapters ago, but slightly different. Think of time as a two-way street—if manifestation looks forward, synchronicity surfing looks at the here and now. Once it is noticed, what we choose to do with it is up to us. I have heard that when you experience a lot of synchronicity it means you are on the right path. I think of it more as you are in a certain groove. The key is to notice the groove and figure out where it is heading: Is this the groove you want? These grooves matter because they help us see what track we are on. Think of them as signposts on the road of life.

Pay attention to when you're humming a song and it comes on the radio, notice when you say somebody's name and within a few minutes they appear, notice when you think of some book, or word, or idea, and then suddenly it appears in three or four places the same day. The more you pay attention, the more you will register these events happening.

Most important, though, is how you interpret these random events, aka luck.

The perspective we take, the interpretation we make of life's events, means *everything*. As life happens, how you interpret the story of your life is completely up to you. Day by day, moment by moment. Often so much of life feels outside of our control, but how we choose to interpret the hand that fortune has dealt us, and what we do next, is *always* completely up to us.

I have known happy-go-lucky people for whom every occurrence is a lovely and wonderful experience, and who are constantly surprised at their own good fortune. For this sort of optimistic personality, an unpleasant bit of luck is interpreted as a minor setback and they get on with their day. On the other hand, there are the opposite types, people who seem to careen from one piece of bad luck to the next. I am reminded of a coworker I once had who, every time you saw him, seemed to be having a terrible day. In the space of a week he reported that he had cracked his brandnew smartphone, been dumped by his girlfriend, and then had been hit by a car while crossing the street (breaking his arm). He was fired shortly thereafter. My point is that this poor fellow seemed to have a little black rain cloud of bad luck that followed him around everywhere.

Most of us, of course, are somewhere in the middle. I think the important thing to remember is that it is all a matter of focus. The upbeat lucky person is really just as likely to drop her phone or get dumped as the rest of us, but rather than interpret bad fortune as part of a wider conspiracy of bad luck, the optimist chooses to shrug it off as a relatively minor inconvenience and keep pushing ahead with her life.

In other words, the secret to synchronicity surfing is that we decide how we interpret, explain, and link the random events and signs that come our way, thus creating our own luck. Basically you are very likely to have the kind of day that you expect to have today. You get back what you put out and reap what you sow.

This ancient truth is fundamental throughout history and across cultures; it is the moral of countless fairy tales. How many versions of the fairy tale exist where three brothers go out in search of their fortune? The first two brothers fail at whatever the quest is because they are selfish and self-centered. And they are usually turned into stone by an ogre or something of that sort. Then the third brother leaves the house and walks down the same path his two elder brothers tried. He is naive by comparison to his brothers. He shares his lunch with a nest of hungry birds, he helps an old crone across a river, he lends his cloak to a dirty old beggar. But when he gets to the ogre's castle, he is aided across the castle walls by the grateful birds, he is given sage advice by the old lady he helped, who was really a powerful sorceress, and the beggar turns out to be a mighty king in disguise, who gives him a magic sword, and so on. The particulars always vary, but the story is essentially the same. The young man who optimistically helped others, expecting nothing in return, is aided by those he helped and thus he is able to defeat the evil ogre, rescue his two brothers, and ultimately win the hand of the princess and a castle full of treasure. Nowadays we have self-help books that tell us to stay positive, but humanity has been teaching its children this basic lesson in stories around the campfire since time immemorial.

The young man of the fairy tale is you. But the two older brothers are also you. All three face the same challenges, but interpret them in different ways, in this most basic of fairy tales that exists in myriad versions. The path traveled by the young hero is each of us, throughout the course of a lifetime, but also in the course of one day.

The first principle of magic is that of correspondence. That the small is mirrored in the large. By this principle, the magus recognizes that *how you live today is how you will live your life.* The foolish brother and the wise brother meet the same challenges and obstacles, but they choose to interpret what they meet along the path in completely different ways.

To put it in plain language, your happiness, indeed your destiny, is entirely up to your interpretation of it. The surrounding circumstances matter a lot less than we might suppose.

18

How to Get Lost

Wandering re-establishes the original harmony which once existed between man and the universe.

—Anatole France

TECHNIQUE

Use an artificial means to get lost. The mind state of being lost produces a brand-new way of seeing things. And forcing yourself to see your surroundings from a new angle can produce unexpected results.

TOOLS REQUIRED

A map of a city that you're not in; Paris, for example
A bicycle
Walking shoes (optional)

TIME REQUIRED

About an hour. More if you really get good and lost! Don't try this at night and bring a phone.

RESULT

Seeing your surroundings with the eyes of a traveler. Making it new.

Here it is! I will tell you the big secret, what it all boils down to, the heart of the matter. You are now ready to grasp the core issue, the fundamental concept of magic to which we will return again and again: *That which is below is as that which is above, and that which is above is as that which is below.*

That's it. The quote is from Hermes Trismegistus.* Rather than get sidetracked with an investigation into the musty pedigree of the quote (a rabbit trail that too many texts on magic become entangled in), we can take that statement—as above so below, and as below so above—as a jumping-off point. On the surface it seems simple enough, almost a tautology. However, like all big truths, it grows in profundity as we approach it.

This idea of correspondence between the above and the below is of course referring to the link between the self and the world, the microcosm and the macrocosm, the interior and the exterior. The accomplished magus realizes that changing the one changes the other. It is as simple and powerful as balancing algebraic equations—what is done on one side must be done on the other.

(In the realm of magic, this law is as basic as Newton's third law of motion, that for every action there is an equal and opposite reaction; it is likewise elegant. Interesting to note: Sir Isaac Newton was himself an alchemist and well familiar with the writings of Trismegistus—even writing his own translation of the *Emerald Tablet*.)

---

* Hermes Trismegistus is a magus of old with a confusing pedigree. While many earnest tomes consider him an actual learned and wise personage who lived in ancient Egypt and authored many Ur-alchemic texts, he is thought by modern scholars to be a representation of the Egyptian god Toth mixed with the Greek god Hermes, representing the flow of arcane Egyptian ideas that helped pollinate the thoughts of the ancient Greeks.

Now let's begin with a basic example—if you were to walk around the block with a pebble in your shoe, it would change not only the way you walk but the way you think and feel. That's too obvious perhaps. Let's zoom back. Picture yourself commuting to work. Do you drive? Then imagine yourself taking the bus. Already take the bus? Imagine if your commute took place by subway or train. Would you like it better, less? If you currently ride the rails, then imagine what it would be like getting there by horse. Now imagine a bicycle. Depending on the distance and route you travel daily, some of these means of transport might sound preferable while others would totally suck. We are affected not only by our environment but also by the way we navigate it, and of course it flows the other way around.

Take your bicycle, for example: What is healthy for us is also healthy for the environment. It is cheap, efficient, and contributes 0 percent pollution. It bears mentioning that at this point in human history, if everyone on earth used a bike as his main mode of transportation, it just might save the ecosystem of the planet. That is the macro level. We could also go down one level and talk about what your hometown or city would look like right now if every car was replaced with a bike; no roads, just trails! Picture how that would change the dynamics of day-to-day life. Roads would be replaced with what? Promenades? Parks? Goat trails? The change in infrastructure this would have on everything from grocery stores and markets to shopping and business centers would be beyond revolutionary.

My point is not to rally you all to tear down urban blight . . . not just yet—but to consider that *change on the micro level proportionally affects the macro*—that is, more bikes = less pavement; that is, everything within us has its repercussions without, and everything perceived in reality its correlative within the individual. The equal sign in the previous statement may be thought of as psychogeography, a term that Guy Debord defined as "the study of the precise laws and specific effects of the geographical environment, consciously organized or not, on the emotions and behavior of individuals."* Debord's version of the following spell was the *dérive*—to drift.

Finally, let us consider the profound effects that biking-not-driving has on oneself: mind, spirit, and body. You travel much more slowly on two wheels than on four. You notice things. The spirit feels the freedom inherent in self-sufficiency as the body is strengthened rather than atrophied. With this in mind, let's take a look at this chapter's magic spell.

---

* From Guy Debord, "Introduction to a Critique of Urban Geography."

HOW TO GET LOST IN PARIS REGARDLESS OF WHERE YOU ARE

This spell will force you to see bits of your macrocosm (ergo, yourself) that you are not used to seeing, as you don't seek them out. If you can become completely lost while performing this spell, then consider yourself an adept—the trick of much magic is to be able to trick yourself.

First step: Get ahold of a map of Paris, or any city that you're not in. Choose a start location and an end location on your map—for example, the Champs-Élysées to the Eiffel Tower, and use the directions as dictated by the map to navigate your way from where you are in your hometown—transposing the navigation of another place onto your current location.

Because you aren't in Paris, you should hopefully be helplessly lost after a few turns. If not, keep going until you are. The map you choose and the directions are incidental, as long as you try to follow a route that is sufficiently complicated. You can even replace the map method with any number of means, such as rolling dice or flipping a coin at each intersection, or better yet, asking strangers for destinations rather than directions.

This experiment works just as well with a group as it does solo. It can, of course, be done on foot as a flâneur as well. It just depends on how much time you have. Really, getting lost on foot, or at least finding yourself in a place you normally wouldn't be, is hard. It's easier on a bike since you travel faster. I can get lost on my bike in less than an hour! While on foot it takes all day. By becoming lost we can more easily observe the connection between our inner state and our surroundings because we see the old with new eyes.

With a little bit of practice, you are ready to experience your environment as though you were a visitor. See it not as a place to traverse but as an environment to explore and experience . . . go as slowly as possible. Unless you'd like to go fast; that's fine too.

19

Meditation

*We hammer wood for a house, but it is the inner space that
makes it livable.* —Tao Te Ching

TECHNIQUE

This simple, free, healthy, and ancient technique can be used by
anyone. Just sit.

TOOLS REQUIRED

None needed, except a quiet place free of distraction.

TIME REQUIRED

A few minutes to start

RESULT

A clear mind, focus, and calm that will radiate outward to affect all parts of your life. While it is one of the simplest techniques in this book, given time it is also one of the most powerful.

Anybody can do it, everybody should. Sit and still your thoughts. Modern books on meditation often recommend that you try it sitting in a chair, but I think sitting cross-legged on the ground is better; it reminds you that you are sitting with purpose. Try to think of nothing. At first this seems impossible. Relax and breathe and let go of your thoughts. There are a lot of different things that you can focus on, mantras and so forth, but the best place to start is just to focus on your breath. Breathe in and out, and notice your breath; calmly let all thoughts come and go. Watch them as they pass by, but don't invite them to sit down with you! Eventually your thoughts begin to fall away, a stream in the background, and an inner clarity will grow within you, day by day, as you practice.

Begin with just a few minutes a day. Like physical exercise, it's counterproductive to overdo it at first. Start slow, there is no rush; it is meant to be a lifelong practice. Slowly work up to fifteen or twenty minutes a day. From there, you will likely want to lengthen as you progress, because the effects are beautiful.

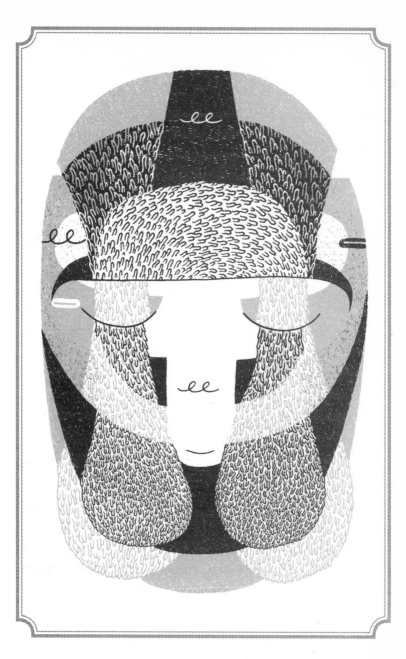

20

Dreamtime & Astral Projection

The world of imagination is the world of eternity. It is the divine bosom into which we shall all go after the death of the vegetated body. This world of imagination is infinite and eternal, whereas the world of generation is finite and temporal. There exist in that eternal world the eternal realities of everything which we see reflected in this vegetable glass of nature.
                                        —William Blake

TECHNIQUE

Navigating the dream world is tricky—first off you have to wake up just a third of the way. With a little practice you will find that you can inhabit the dreaming and the waking world at the same time. Stories of people traveling outside of their bodies while sleeping exist in many cultures; is it just a common dream or something more?

TOOLS REQUIRED

Focus and practice

Naps (It's harder to do this at nighttime because then sleep is heavier.)

It's helpful to have intermittent background noise that will wake you just a little:

- Someone cooking in the kitchen
- Traffic going on outside
- Classical music that rises and falls in volume

TIME REQUIRED

Long enough to take a nap

RESULT

An out-of-body experience!

One thing just about every culture seems to have in common is stories about people traveling out of their bodies. This has many different names in different places; I will simply refer to it here as astral projection because that seems to be its most recent name.

This travel is understood to happen in another place—or to be more precise, it happens in another version of this place.* Ancient philosophers from Plato onward claim that this world is a sort of shadow or echo of a more fundamental world. This idea is also seen in the Cabala, in Hindu scriptures, and it is integral in mysticism everywhere from Christianity, to Islam, to Taoist and Hindu legends. The prophets and heroes of the Old Testament were often informed by dreams, while in the Koran the prophet Muhammad travels many miles in a single night to lead others in prayer, and in Buddhist tradition monks travel while asleep to impart messages to faraway friends. Attempts at traveling outside of the body have also been explored and documented by mystics such as Emanuel Swedenborg, Hereward Carrington, and Robert Monroe and even the popular author Michael Crichton. The idea that one can travel outside of oneself to a spirit realm is also seen in the teachings of older shamanic cultures and the Australian Aboriginal concept of dreamtime.

What these many cultures and viewpoints agree on is that this form of *travel* happens in another *place*. For the sake of simplicity I refer here to that travel as astral projection and that place as dreamtime. Rather than me telling you some theory or dogma

---

* The other place has also been called, for example, the ethereal plane, dreamtime, faerie, Swarga Loga, the spirit realm, the astral plane, Summerland, Emain Ablach (the fortress of apples), Arūpyadhātu (the formless realm), Annwfn, and Tír na nÓg.

about what this place the Aborigines called dreamtime objectively is, I think it better if I simply tell you how to experience it for yourself.

The most straightforward method is to attempt to wake up your mind while your body stays asleep, but I warn that it is also a particularly hard state to conjure up.* It seems closely related to the phenomenon of sleep paralysis.

The easiest way to begin is to drift off to sleep, but then have some sort of background noise half wake you up. I recommend classical music, which can lull you to sleep but also has periods of crescendo. I have also noticed that it helps if you sleep in a room with the lights on; if it is dark it is difficult to tell you are not simply dreaming. You will need to experiment to find what works for you.

There is a motor control, muscle inhibition paralysis that occurs when you enter REM sleep; otherwise you would respond to the contents of your dreams by flopping and flailing about and quite likely hurt yourself. If you manage to half wake up, but not fully, then while bobbing in and out of sleep, a fragment of your consciousness can become aware of being in your sleeping body and the room around you, ambient sounds and vision, and so on,

---

* Other methods include various forms of meditation, and more recently people have been experimenting with binaural beats: trance induced by listening to certain frequencies with headphones.

while the body itself is still unable to move. It is this weird limbo state that can be used as the takeoff runway for astral projection.

The reason more people don't access this more often is because it feels weird and a little scary. You are awake, but you can't move at all, and if you fight the feeling it can be quite wrenching; you can become overwhelmed by a sensation of being trapped, paralyzed, and helpless. Most people fight it and freak out, and it becomes an unpleasant thing to be avoided. Once you recognize it to be harmless, it presents much less of a challenge.

The next step takes even a bit more awareness. All the same, I believe that with intention and practice anybody can do it. At this point, you want to become conscious enough of the sleep paralysis state to explore it a bit. Your inner dialogue can go something like, "Hey . . . I'm in my body, and I can't move, well that's weird, but I'm aware and thinking." If you freak out, then you will get uptight and jerk yourself awake, and if you relax too much, then you will just slip right back into sleep, so it's a balancing act, like surfing a wave; you gotta combine a steely determination with the loosey-goosey wiles of an old stoner surf wizard.

When you reach that sweet spot of being kinda awake but your body is quite numb and unmoving, you may notice a loud whooshing, roaring noise, like the static of a radio tuned to a dead station mixed with a cacophony of unintelligible voices, which I believe to be a taste of madness. If you're able to ride past that threshold without being startled awake, then congratulations. You've done it.

You will notice that you are conscious in the sleep-frozen body that you identify as yourself, but there actually is a bit of wiggle room within the cockpit of selfness. Your own personal point of view is stretchy at this stage, basically like Silly Putty, and if you play around just a little bit, with intention you can, without moving your physical body, stretch the POV out of your body and float around.

Yup, that's pretty much it. Where you go from there is up to you. You can just kind of float in the direction you think of. If you look at, say, an object on a table, you will inevitably drift over toward it until it fills your entire frame of reference.

Does the geography of dreamtime shift and change depending on who enters into its lands and by what means? It seems to me analogous to the invisible color spectrum; we know that the human eye can see just a small portion of the electromagnetic spectrum (from red to blue), and there are other frequencies invisible to us, yet ubiquitous all around us.

21

Power Stance

People pay to see others believe in themselves.
—Kim Gordon of Sonic Youth

TECHNIQUE

Learn how to use the posture of your body to affect how you feel and how others see you. Start with the four basic postures and then create your own.

TOOLS REQUIRED

A private room where you can try these postures out. If you're at home that's one thing, but a bathroom stall works; a nearby park bench or small plot of grass is great too.

D.I.Y. Magic

TIME REQUIRED

5 to 10 minutes

RESULT

Increased confidence, self-esteem, and feelings of relaxation and self-autonomy. One of the best bang-for-your-buck tricks in the book. Once you try this, I am sure you will use it often.

&

Recently, scientific research has once again demonstrated something that ancient traditions have been saying for millennia: that the posture of our bodies can affect the way we feel. Amy Cuddy, a social psychologist at Harvard, has studied the way people react to holding different postures or stances. She found that holding power stances increased confidence. What's a power stance? It's a posture of expansiveness and spread-out largesse.

We all look big when we feel confident and small when we are feeling defensive and submissive. Compare an open stance posture with a closed-off posture—arms crossed and folded up instead of loose and relaxed, posture slumped down instead of upright and alert—the difference is immediate not just in how these postures feel but how they look to others.

For a power stance, any pose that is open and spread out works. The interesting thing is that once you pay attention to how you feel in these different poses, you will notice that you can actually just make up your own poses and body language and read the effects they are having on your emotions, all on your own. Try it. The connection is simple: The way we hold ourselves strongly affects the way we feel. Would you like to feel more confident or happier or more powerful or less stressed? It can be as simple as looking more confident, happier, relaxed.

You can use power stances to give yourself a boost anytime you need it. It just takes a few minutes to work and doesn't require any special gear or training. It is especially effective for situations like going into a job interview, speaking in front of a crowd, asking somebody out on a date, or whenever you need to do anything for which you could use a little boost of confidence.

After becoming comfortable with this technique, you might find that you pay more attention to the way your posture affects how you feel in general. Mastering the basic power stances can be just the beginning. You can try different postures or asanas. You can make up your own. You can control how you feel from the outside in. And you can easily see how this simple little trick can be a great thing to have handy whenever you need it!

Feeling confident translates to making you more laid-back and stress free. Not only will power stances make it easier for you to handle whatever situation you are heading into that requires confidence but it also will be subtly noticed by other people as well; on a subconscious level they will see you as more confident and therefore competent. This creates an upward spiral.

Here are four power postures to try:

- Standing with your legs wide apart, hands firmly on hips, elbows pointing out. Think of Superman or Wonder Woman.

- Propping your legs up on a desk or table, hands folded behind your head. I love this one; it's both empowering and relaxing—and perfect for daydreaming!

- Sitting with one leg crossed over the other in a nonchalant way, while perhaps draping an arm across the back of a nearby chair or whatever is at hand. This confident posture is one that fits comfortably over anything and everything around it.

- And I'll just add this one myself—I don't think it's been studied: You ever notice how lying on the ground, legs and arms outstretched wide, feels very refreshing and invigorating?

22

Surreal Juxtaposition

Good artists copy, great artists steal.
—Anon*

TECHNIQUE

Take old ideas, images, or sounds and give them new life, in a new context. Borrow, copy, steal, and recombine to make something fresh. These games were popular with the Dadaists and helped inspire a revolution in art. Find out what you can do with them.

---

* This quote is often mistakenly attributed to Picasso, but he never actually said it, so I don't know which artist I'm stealing this quote from.

TOOLS REQUIRED

Scissors
Glue
Tape
Old magazines
Photographs
Books
A typewriter

TIME REQUIRED

An afternoon

RESULT

A recombination of old parts that create something new synergistically = a whole that is greater than the sum of its parts.

※

With their collage art (an image of, say, a lobster/airplane with human arms), the Dadaists and surrealists were the harbingers of the art of juxtaposition. Currently, the art of juxtaposing different mediums is exploding. YouTube and the Internet are rife with it:

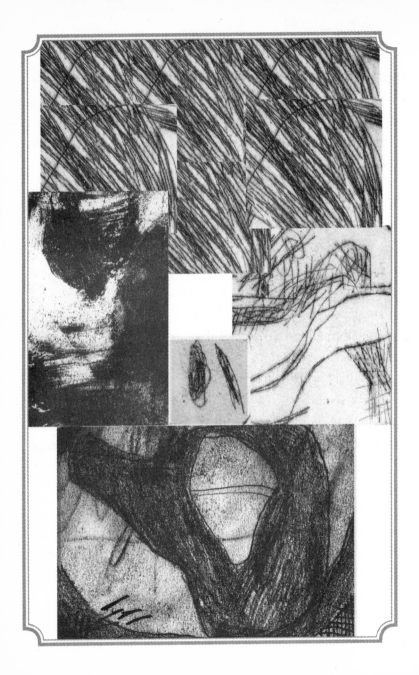

Surreal Juxtaposition

Cutups and blended together Photoshopped pics and video, music mashups, and the use of Auto-Tune have turned everybody into a burgeoning surrealist. However, you don't need to be an Internet artist—you can practice surreal juxtaposition in everyday life as well.

The classic trick is to watch *The Wizard of Oz* with the sound turned down while playing *The Dark Side of the Moon*. Yes, it helps to be high for that one. (Hell, come to think of it, that probably holds true for much of this book! But trust me, it's not completely necessary. I get by fine mostly on caffeine myself.) But there is no reason to limit yourself to that one classic combo. Experiment with different films and soundtracks. *Scooby-Doo* and the Beatles. Jodorowsky and Beethoven. *Star Wars* and hip-hop. The potential combinations are limitless.

And that's just film. You can also try it in real life. Put on some headphones and go downtown and people watch, and now, if you can sync it up just perfectly . . .

Here are a few other surrealist tricks and parlor games you can try. Are they art? Are they just games? Is there a difference?

- **Exquisite Corpse.** Fold a paper in thirds and draw a creature. One person draws the head, another the torso, a third the feet, all without viewing each other's drawings until it is finished.

- **Questions & Answers.** Fold a few small slips of paper in half. On the top half one person writes some questions, one for each paper. On the bottom another person writes some answers, without looking at the questions. When both people are in the right frame of mind, the results can be poetic and edifying.

- **The Naked Lunch Method.** Take a newspaper or a page from a book and create a new text by cutting it up and pasting it back together.

- **Collage.** Paste together fragments of found pictures.

- **Proverbs for Today.** Every player tries to invent a new saying or proverb.

- **Bulletism.** Spray drops of ink on a blank piece of paper. Then use the droplets as the basis for creating a drawing.

- **Dream Résumé.** Make a résumé of things that you have done in your dreams. It should highlight your strengths, experiences, objectives, and skills. For example, your dream experiences might include flying, talking to animals, and eating pizza with Abraham Lincoln. Print your dream résumé out and be sure to update it from time to time.

Surreal Juxtaposition

- **Time Traveler's Christmas.** Ask each player, If you could visit any person throughout history, what gift would you bring him or her and why? The gifts can be as serious or silly as you like.

- **Latent News.** Take a newspaper, cut out words and phrases, and rearrange them to make a poem.

- **Homolinguistic Translation.** Take a poem and translate it from English to English. So you might translate the words into synonyms or into slang. It is like a game of telephone. Give this new poem to someone else and have her repeat the process. With each translation, the poem will mutate into something else.

- **Make Up Your Own . . .**

The revolution we carry inside us will not look like us: so different is it that we hesitate to bring it into the world. —Alain Jouffroy

23

The Flâneur

All truly great thoughts are conceived while walking.
—Friedrich Nietzsche

TECHNIQUE

Appreciate life from a different pace, a different angle; notice the details and see what you're missing when you're in a car. Where are you going, and what's the big hurry? Why walk when you can stroll, mosey, and lollygag? Can walking be a way of life, a philosophy . . . and much more fun than traveling by car?

TOOLS REQUIRED

A comfortable pair of shoes
More often than not, an umbrella
A notebook, if you like

TIME REQUIRED

Probably longer than you think

RESULT

This is not so much about the result as the thing itself. The journey is the destination.

Flâneur is French for "walker," "saunterer," or "loafer." But to say a flâneur is someone who just goes for walks is like saying a chef is someone who just makes food. Walking, to the flâneur, is an art form. The flâneur walks; I should say he also moseys, strolls, wanders, lollygags, idles, and loafs as well as saunters and sashays. Flâneurs see walking in the city as a mode of self-expression and exploration. They might walk in order to think, but they are just as likely to space out and daydream about nothing in particular.

It is a most useful art for appreciating life and for taking in the world. Flâneurs are likely to people watch, car watch, and bird-watch; building, window, fashion, and cloud watch. They appreciate everything as it passes by.

The art of walking does not require a great deal of seriousness, and the flâneur is always free to pause to chat with other strollers and loafers and perhaps to flirt, to gossip or tell stories, to smell the roses, to roll about in the roil of urban life, and to brazenly gawk at the world. A flâneur understands that walking is not just about getting somewhere; the act of walking can be its own reward, pleasurable, relaxing, and fun. One can be a true flâneur only in the city. If you try to be a flâneur in the forest, it is something quite different; it is hiking.

What is the difference between the hiker and the flâneur? you might ask. Aren't they both just walking about? Ah, yes, on the surface they appear very similar. The difference is that the hiker goes to escape from society and civilization and seeks some peace and quiet amid the trees, whereas the flâneur revels and wallows in society and civilization; the flâneur is as much an exhibit as a looker. The flâneur is one who appreciates looking at everything, and because of this the flâneur tends to dress well. It is a give-and-take. "Look at me, I'm walking!" the flâneur says.

I want to point out two other important qualities to being a flâneur. One, it is revolutionary. We live in a world created, designed, and maintained for cars, but the flâneur insists on traveling by foot, refusing to take the world on the terms dictated by technology and choosing to slow things down to an older and more natural way of travel. It seems strange that we let the environment of our cities shape us instead of the other way around. I grew up in a landscape of suburban sprawl. People hardly ever walked anywhere because the sidewalks were ugly—crowded with fast-food chains, billboards, and the noxious fumes and noise of passing trucks. But if more people were walkers, it seems it could be the other way. What would cities look like if walking were commonplace and cars unusual?

Even more important than the fact that walking can reshape our environment, walking reshapes ourselves. The way we think while going on a walk becomes calmer, deeper, more insightful, and more meditative. There is a quality to the thoughts that come while walking that is unlike any other mode of thinking. Many of the world's most original thinkers were huge lovers of walking. Beethoven would take a long walk every day, rain or shine, to compose his music in his head. Other prodigious daily walkers include Einstein, Erik Satie, Beckett, Darwin, Tchaikovsky, Steve Jobs, Thoreau, Aristotle, Charles Dickens, and Goethe.

To be a flâneur, appreciate everything as it passes by on your walk. The art of walking does not require a great deal of seriousness, and you are always free to stop for a moment when the mood strikes. To be a flâneur is to be always open to trying a new route, to exploring a new side street or a path.

Sometimes the flâneur will spend an hour or two in a café drinking tea or Americanos and, as often as not, smoking. But this is just a break, for the flâneur's true passion is aimlessly ambling about.

Perhaps walking is so good for our thoughts and brains because in its rhythmic circumlocution it mirrors the rhythms and vicissitudes of human thought. If you pay attention to the flow of your own thoughts, you can easily see that the speed, quality, and focus of one's thoughts change depending on what activity you are doing. Thoughts while running, for example, are often hurried and hard to remember. Your thinking changes depending on whether you are driving a car, riding a bike, sitting still in a chair, or chopping up vegetables with a knife. There is probably something to be said for each of these different ways of being and how they affect concentration. But walking is the best for thinking. This is the secret of the flâneur. Walking propels our thoughts to keep up in rhythm, to move from idea to idea, neither too fast nor too slow, as the landscape changes before our eyes, as new visual stimuli introduce new inspiration to the flow of our thoughts. Walking provides solitude and gets us away from daily distractions. It gets the blood flowing to the brain, and keeps our thoughts lively. The flâneur walks not just to get from point A to B. Walking is a form of contemplation. The flâneur walks to be more fully human.

24

Active Imagination

Many poets and all mystics and occult writers, in all ages and countries, have declared that behind the visible are chains and chains of conscious beings who are not of heaven but are of earth, who have no inherent form, but change according to their whim, or the mind that sees them. —W. B. Yeats

TECHNIQUE

Treat the imagination as a real place. Taking the imagination seriously, as a real thing, gives it power, vitality, and meaning.

TOOLS REQUIRED

A spacious and stretchy mind
A strong imagination or a willingness to strengthen the
imagination by practice

TIME REQUIRED

An eternity, since we lose track of time when swept away by
imagination.

RESULT

A new way of seeing the world. A limitless wellspring of creativity.

During the golden age of Islam it was believed that a world exists
between the physical realm and the divine called *'ālam al-mithāl*,
the imaginal world. The great Persian philosopher Avicenna ex-
plained that imagination worked as a sort of mediator or translator
between the human realm and the spiritual. The divine could
reach down through this imaginal world to shape and sustain the
physical world, and humans could reach up through the imaginal
to attain visions of the sublime. This line of thinking is seen in

many places; it is apparent in the philosophy of Plato, and Goethe, and in mystics such as Jacob Böhme as well as poets like Coleridge and Blake.

Imagination can give us access to a real place that is more than just the subjective fantasy of the individual. On the surface this seems like a very bold and controversial idea; it flies in the face of everything that we now accept in our logical and scientific world-view. And yet it pops up again and again, in so many places—in philosophy, in literature, even in science. Some of the biggest scientific discoveries were the result of experiments in the imagination; for example, Einstein used imaginary thought experiments to discover his theory of relativity.*

The kind of imagination these thinkers are referring to is active imagination, which is different from the common daydream. Active imagination involves visiting a realm of imagination that is receptive to inspiration. It is a state of openness, of being open to whatever ideas form, and of letting the imagination take control.

Artists, poets, writers, and creators often speak of it, although everyone uses different language for it. Writers like Coleridge and Blake speak of the process of going to the realm of the imagination as if it were an actual place; the ideas and imagery they find there

---

* Other famous thought experiments include Schrödinger's cat, Laplace's demon, Newton's cannonball, the twin paradox, Avicenna's falling man, and the ship of Theseus.

are not just things they have made up, they are things they have discovered. The director David Lynch speaks of ideas as being out there like fishes, as though the creative ideas exist somehow on their own; therefore, to catch a big fish/idea you have to go to the deeper watering holes.

Active imagination is a sustained imagining that builds something real, something that is true because it is built from what Jung called the archetypal, meaning truths that are true not just for any given person, but for all people. It is because of active imagination that any art, be it a painting or a movie or a book, has real meaning and is more than just the fantasy of the individual. A work of art that has been created through active imagination resonates for everyone. This magical realm is also what makes some music feel inspired. In flamenco it is called duende, and in the blues it is soul. Imagination is perhaps the quintessential human activity; cats, crows, and octopuses can all use reason to some extent after all.

Let me be clear, active imagination is more than just a skill. It is a doorway to a place. A real place. A place we all visited frequently in childhood. The path to this place can become overgrown and hard to find as adults. You might consider this book as a machete, designed to help you clear the way through these overgrown paths, to regain access to the realm of the imagination.

With all of this in mind, I suggest we turn to Jung's concept of active imagination. For Jung, who coined the term *active imagination*, it was a process of expressing the unconscious. Jung spoke of the

active imagination as being a bridge between the self and the unconscious—access to another realm via the imagination. Jung discovered his version of active imagination while studying alchemy. He realized that what the alchemists were talking about was actually the same psychological process that he had been studying his whole life, the relationship between the self and the other realm—what he called the collective unconscious. So how exactly did Jung go about accessing his active imagination? Simple: He played, like a child.

We know from his autobiography that as an old man, Jung spent a great deal of time simply playing make-believe in his backyard. He made a sort of sandbox on his property and played with rocks, creating patterns and sandcastle-like structures, constructing model buildings, being guided by his subconscious, and generally behaving like an eight-year-old! It was directly after he began this work that he was flooded with the archetypal imagery that became the wellspring of his life's work (Jung's *Red Book*). This was not easy at all for Jung to do, who said it was a "painfully humiliating experience to realize that there was nothing to be done but play childish games."*

There are no laid-in-stone steps for accessing your active imag-

---

* Besides playing in a sandbox, Jung would often sit still in a chair and allow himself to actively daydream and visualize whatever came to mind; he would later carefully draw what he saw.

ination. You can simply pretend you are a child and play make-believe, being guided by only your imagination. For Jung, this meant playing with rocks. For another person, it may be found in art. The main key is to strike a balance between the imagination and the ego.

SOME PRACTICAL TIPS FOR USING ACTIVE IMAGINATION

Your active imagination is a state of mind, of trusting the process of make-believe. Jung stressed the importance of letting the imagination take its course. Think of your imagination as a horse that knows its way: Guide it a little, but give it free rein to wander where it pleases. It is a dance, not a wrestling match; it cannot be forced or faked. It is the process of tapping into something real, something larger than your own ideas, the source of creativity itself. It is why writers speak of their characters coming alive. When a person has writer's block it is usually because she is trying to force her way into the realm of the active imagination.

The key principle to accessing your active imagination is to take imagination seriously. To allow it to deepen and travel far. It is not something to be taken lightly; throughout history the practice of it has been seen as sacred and sometimes a great burden, and possibly even dangerous if misused. It is easy to shrug off any strange, silly, or whimsical notion that comes to us from the imagination as "just a daydream." But it is when we follow these fanciful thoughts and play with them that we allow the imagination to take control. What this means exactly to you will depend on what you're doing. As a writer it means allowing yourself to be surprised by what the characters you are writing say and do, to be surprised by where the line you are typing takes you.

In any art form, active imagination is that moment of allowing the raw imagination to take over; it is the comedian doing improv with no script in front of a live mic, it is the guitarist jamming a solo, the jazz pianist vamping on top of the melody, the rapper freestyling over a beat, the entrepreneur taking a risk on a hunch, the filmmaker who keeps the camera rolling while the actors improvise right in the moment, the painter following the whim of the brush right there on the canvas with no preconceived image. It is discovering the beauty of the thing you are trying to do while you are in the process of doing it: no script, no safety net, 100 percent live, just winging it, spontaneous and free. It is how to always make it fresh and new, whatever it is you are doing. In one word: *play*.

Do not dismiss your impulses, follow them! Taking the imagination seriously is necessary if we are to learn to listen to it, to be open to what it reveals, rather than trying to force our own desires and wishes upon it.

25

Memento Mori

Death makes life meaningless because everything we have ever striven for ceases when life does, and it makes life meaningful, too, because its presence makes the little we have of it indispensable, every moment precious.

—Karl Ove Knausgaard

TECHNIQUE

Remember your own mortality in order to live better.

TOOLS REQUIRED (PICK ONE)

A moth (symbol of the soul)
Something green (symbol of death in medieval culture)
Something black

A pomegranate

An hourglass

A fossil

Scrimshaw

Lilies

A scarab

A statue or bust of a famous dead person

A snake

A painting or poster

An animal skull or skeleton

A crow or an owl

A cross

A wheel (a symbol of death and rebirth in Buddhism)

A picture of a sunset

TIME REQUIRED

This one isn't a one-shot deal; it is a symbol that you select to remind yourself of the facts, in the same way a wristwatch, a wedding ring, a bathroom scale, or a sticky note can.

RESULT

A fuller appreciation of life, gained by cultivating an awareness of death.

Hey, you there! Could I please have your attention for a moment? Yes, you, right there, the reader. No, don't look over your shoulder; I'm not talking to the person behind you. I'm not talking to the person who might have read this sentence before or after you. I mean precisely you. I have a message for you specifically that is going to come true. I will be blunt. Ready?

You are going to die.

There, I said it. Now calm down; I'm not saying anything you didn't already know. I'm just reminding you of something that you already knew. You will die. It's a fact. I will too. We all will. We don't know how or when, but it is inevitable. It's also something that we are supposed to pretend to forget, apparently. At least in Western culture, you don't hear a whole lot about mortality these days. Like it's not a big deal. Well, it *is* a big deal! Everything that you know here, in this life, it will all end. This life is not a practice run, it's not a dress rehearsal, this is it!

Before you sidle away from me and my rant here, like I'm a bug-eyed, wild-haired crazy person who is accosting you on the street, let me defend myself and say that there is a long, rich history of people who thought it very important to remind themselves and others, once in a while, that we humans don't get to live forever. Granted, a lot of them were monks and philosophers, who tend to be a gloomy bunch. But the awareness of one's own mortality does not have to be morbid. I believe that it can be inspiring, uplifting, and help remind you of your focus and purpose. A memento mori is an object that is meant to remind you that someday you will die. The phrase is Latin for "remember that you will die." It is necessary because these days we tend to live as though death were not true, as though we could forget about it. Talk of death is viewed as unpleasant, and it is seen as rude to bring it up. Nowadays, in a world oft driven by commercialism and capitalism, the message is, "Don't worry about the end, chill out and drink a Coke, watch some TV, forget about it. If you feel worried or unsatisfied, maybe you should buy something?"

I maintain that death is not morbid, it is natural, it is simply the state of things, and reminding yourself that you will one day die is no more weird and morbid than reminding yourself that you cannot fly. Indeed, if we often forgot that we can't fly, we would want to write that fact down on a card and keep it in our pocket, no? Just as medieval philosophers would often keep a human skull as a memento mori on their desktop to remind themselves that they would one day die.

When you begin each day knowing that it is a unique opportunity, that this day has never happened before in human history and will never happen again, then you take it seriously. Do you think that in being aware of death you will be kinder or more selfish? Will you be more or less likely to reach for your goals and dreams when you remind yourself that this is a one-shot deal? Of course we can't be like the medieval philosopher and keep an actual human skull on our desks. Memento mori can be anything that reminds you that life is fleeting, that existence is temporal. I use an hourglass. I keep it on my desk, and it reminds me that time spent does not come back. Your personal memento mori can be a drawing, a photograph, an object, an hourglass, a piece of jewelry, whatever works for you. For some people it can be something forceful like a skull; for others it could be something more subtle like a picture of a moth or a candle, as long as you know what it means. Choose whatever speaks to you.

It can even just be a phrase that you write down and keep somewhere. It is said that Solomon wore a ring that read "this too shall pass." When he was sad it made him happy, and when he was happy it made him sad. Set up your own memento mori somewhere that your glance will fall upon at least once a day. And whenever you notice it, let it remind yourself—this is it. Now, make it count!

26

Counting Coup

Life shrinks or expands in proportion to one's courage.
—Anaïs Nin

TECHNIQUE

Use what scares you to make you stronger. The more we face things that make us afraid, the braver we become.

TOOLS REQUIRED

Anything that is kind of scary

TIME REQUIRED

Just a few seconds, as long as they are the kind of seconds where time slows down.

RESULT

Guts. Cojones. Brass. Grit. Courage. Bravery doesn't mean you're not afraid, it means you face your fears and own them.

Having recently survived a jaw-rattling, RV-sideswiping, ocean cliffside–edged, eight-hundred-mile bicycling trip along the Pacific coast, from Portland to San Francisco, my thoughts have been turning inward toward the concept of honor and danger. It is an old idea: We must stand at the edge of safety and comfort and flirt with the possibility of death to fully recognize the boundaries of life.

The Plains Indians practiced the art of counting coup. To count coup, you must sneak up to an enemy warrior and touch him with a coup stick . . . and then run for your life! This ritualized combat had little to do with warfare as we understand it in modern terms. The point was not to kill or incapacitate the enemy (although by counting coup, the warrior demonstrated he could have van-

quished the foe if he had wanted), and therefore it had nothing to do with the modern point of an attack: lessening the forces of the other side. It was instead a form of warfare on a personal level. But do not make the mistake of thinking this merely some sort of game! The stakes for counting coup were exactly life and death. This is what gave the act its meaning and power. Honor was once seen as a very real thing and as something that could be strengthened, fostered, and grown by one's own feats. Each warrior who was tagged with a coup stick earned one notch on the stick for the bearer.

Nowadays deadly enemy warriors can be a scarcity, but it is still possible to skillfully tread a line that flirts with risk and danger, and learn from the doing. The simplest example I can think of (short of running up to a group of tough-looking strangers, smacking one on the head with a stick, and then running) is to find the biggest, steepest hill in your town and then bomb down it on a bicycle without using brakes . . . but there is an infinite number of ways to count coup.

I can imagine, my gentle readers, some of you may protest— What!? How is this to be considered magic!? Slapping strangers? Bombing down hills? This sounds more like a bad episode of *Jackass*. Point taken, but keep in mind that magic is a much larger and more holistic system than we might at first give it credit for and also that both honor and magic are very ancient concepts, ones that to some degree modern civilization has lost touch with, but that I believe to be interrelated. On a simplistic level, when we talk of magic, we often are talking about ways of reconnecting to lost and archaic ways of life.

Of course the idea of honor (a real thing that may grow or lessen according to one's feats throughout life) extends beyond something just practiced by the Plains Indians. It has been a primary attribute of primitive cultures—and by "primitive," I mean cultures without guns, where combat and war took place on a personal level. Across cultures and history, in all of our oldest literature, from Beowulf to Charlemagne, from Gilgamesh to King Arthur, to Odysseus defiantly shouting at the blinded Cyclops—we see tales of honor, tales of the hero attempting to gain personal power and renown through acts of bravery—that is to say through acts of survival. The lesson is repeated again and again: You are the sum of your actions. Nothing more, nothing less.

This is a fairly alien concept to us in Western commercial capitalism because we are taught we *are* our clothes, our food, our cigarette and shoe brands, the music we listen to, the car we drive, and so on. Had that always been the case, Homer's *Odyssey* would have featured lots of lengthy chapters detailing what rad sandals the hero wore and what great mileage he got in his luxury-class, leather-interior warship. Modern media claims that you are what you buy. All the old legends say *you are what you survive.*

In honor of this dictum, here is a modernized ritual of counting coup: Simply do something genuinely a bit dangerous! The following are some examples to consider. *Note:* This list is just to give you an idea or two; really anything that involves the possibility of serious injury and/or possibly death works fine—but be careful, the point is to survive, obviously!

Wilderness survival

Skateboarding

Wearing a cardigan and matching bow tie to an Insane Clown Posse concert

Zoobombing (bicycling down the tallest hill available at the fastest speed possible)

Fear and loathing in Las Vegas

Rock climbing

Urban climbing (I have had great experiences with water towers, but smokestacks are much more surreal)

Urban exploration

Public protest

Boxing

The running of the bulls

Riding chicken buses in South America

Breaking up bar fights

Being in bar fights

Rodeo clowning

Growing up being yourself in a small rural town

Let's take a closer look at one of the examples: urban exploration. This is the fine art of breaking into somewhere and having yourself a look-see. Generally the focus is on large and uninhabited spaces, often subterranean; also skyscrapers, sporting venues, tunnels, airports, abandoned factories. Buildings that are not in use, either because they have been shut down or sometimes because they are still under construction, are usually the best. The counting coup is often twofold: Not only must you outwit the authorities, but since the buildings are usually in disrepair and this is generally a nighttime activity, you also risk serious injury at every turn. (Although I have had success getting past security in the daytime by impersonating a delivery person.) Know when to use stealth and know when to hide, but also know when to run!

The classic place for urban exploring is a trip to the lower world via tunnels. Many large cities have a forbidden underground that is perfect for urban spelunking: New York, Seattle, Portland, Buenos Aires, Sydney, Beijing, Paris, Barcelona, Atlanta, and Houston all have extensive underground tunnels, and most large compounds, such as universities, have large series of underground catacombs. And chances are if you are not near an urban tunnel, you are near a cave somewhere.

I recommend trying this with a friend or two, and choose people you can count on not to lose their cool. While exploring an underground viaduct beneath Portland, I was surprised at the

potency of being deep underground and the power with which it affects the psyche. In the pitch darkness, cut off from the officially "sanctioned and safe" reality, what is real quickly becomes mutable. Interesting things happen to the mind when you can't see your hand in front of your face. We all began to hear a strange, faint, and steady thrumming that was inexplicable. After a long distance underground (and still continuing to descend at a steady pace), with the eyes totally dilated but blind, a strange phenomenon begins to happen—you can sense with your eyes. There is a feeling of thickness on a spatial level if you hold your fingers in front of your face or somebody stops in front of you.

After traversing several blocks underground, my companions and I began to get the fear, a sort of inscrutable paranoia. The illusion presented itself so that, rather than a tunnel, we were surrounded on all sides by an endless void. The possibility of a chasm seemed to loom in the darkness, or the possibility that a viaduct somewhere had opened and was flooding up with crashing water, and there lurked the sentiment that somewhere in the darkness was a presence. . . . Of course these fears, and the shared feelings of paranoia, were exactly the point! The thing to be faced—to not panic, to conquer the fears of claustrophobia and darkness, to overcome the fear of the unknown and unfamiliar—is exactly what you gain from such an experience. We marched through the darkest portion of the underground river with spirits high, singing a cappella, our voices stretched out and reverberating to infinity by the endless echoing walls, coming back to us as some strange and alien sound, something impossible to hear or ever experience above ground. Then, satisfied with our exploration, we returned home.

Urban exploration isn't the only way to go. Take, for example, Bill Soder, a fellow I met on my recent bicycle trip while camping in the redwoods. At the age of fifty-three, he has been pitting himself against the adventures of the road and the wild continuously for eight straight years—bicycling from state to state, carrying everything he owns, and camping night after night.

Before he started, he was terribly overweight and sickly and suffering from regular seizures. One of those cases for which the doctor pronounces, "The end is near." One day while watching TV, he was seized with the inspiration to ride his bike into town for a cup of coffee. He told his son he was going to bike into town and his son scoffed, "C'mon, Dad, you're too lazy and fat to make it into town." Whereupon he vowed, "I'll make it to the coffee shop—not only that, I'm gonna bike to the original Starbucks in Seattle . . . and get a fucking cappuccino!"

Since he had never done any bike touring before, and he lived in Boston, this statement was an intention of counting coup. Thousands of miles later, he called his son from the Starbucks in Seattle and had the barista confirm his location and order. Since then he has lost a ton of weight and is feeling in better health than he has his entire life, and he says he is also happier now than he has ever been. He has cycled coast to coast a few times, has been up and down the Pacific innumerable times, and has (in his fifties) explored the deserts of New Mexico and the snowy mountain peaks of the Cascades, all of which his doctors would have pronounced impossible for a man with his conditions. He had grown through his actions.

You are not the clothes you wear. You are not the car you drive. You are not what you eat. You are not the music you listen to. You are not the shows you watch. You are not anything that you can buy, own, wear, sell, steal, or fake. You are what you do.

27

Aleatory Writing

I am trying to be unfamiliar with what I am doing.
—John Cage

TECHNIQUE

Harness chance/chaos to make your writing more lifelike and interesting. (This can also be applied to music, art, and even cooking.) At random places, let pure chance take the steering wheel to open up a new world of possibilities. Sometimes the most beautiful turn of events can be found only by blind luck.

TOOLS REQUIRED (PICK ONE)

Dice
Coins

Aleatory Writing

The *I Ching*
Tarot cards
A stack of random photos
Words picked at random from the dictionary
A willingness to let go

TIME REQUIRED

Just a few minutes for this cantrip

RESULT

A surprise twist to anything you are working on.

The classic example of aleatory writing—writing dependent on the element of chance—can be found in Philip K. Dick's 1962 masterpiece *The Man in the High Castle.** The characters in this multilayered novel frequently consult the *I Ching*, and at each point where the characters cast the *I Ching*, the author would do so as

---

* The concept of aleatory composing is also a familiar idea in music, in the works of John Cage and *The Disintegration Loops* of William Basinksi, for example.

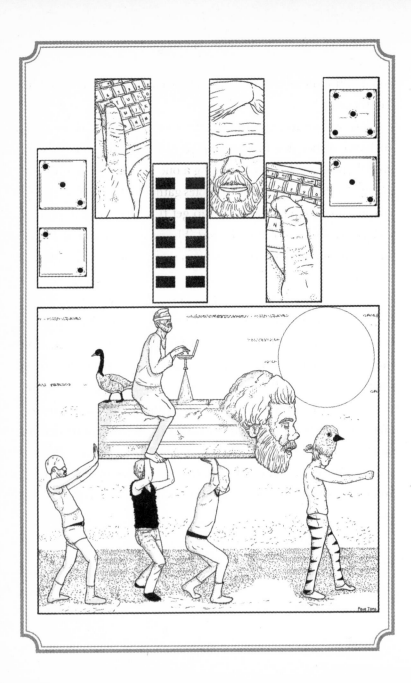

well and use the results to determine what would happen next in the story.

However, aleatory writing need not be as complex as this. Any stochastic device that affects the plot or word choice can be used, from flipping a coin to, say, writing a one-act play while sitting in a crowded café and working in quotes gathered from conversations surrounding you. The idea isn't to get the hypothetical monkey with a typewriter to retype *Hamlet*. The idea is to harness the nature of chaos and to introduce a bit of that chaotic nature into the writing.

The element of chance can be applied in a variety of ways. If you are working on a piece of fiction, you could flip a coin or draw straws whenever a character is faced with a choice. You can draw random events written on slips of paper from a hat to see what happens next. If composing a piece of music, you could roll dice to see what note is played next. While writing a poem, you might try selecting the next line with eyes closed from a dictionary or a newspaper article.

Let some of the act of creating happen outside of your control, and you will discover ideas you never would have thought of.

28

Memory Exercise

You must live life with the full knowledge that your actions will remain. We are creatures of consequence.

—Zadie Smith

TECHNIQUE

Think of your memory as a muscle—use it or lose it. Here's how: Set aside time to think back to your oldest memory. Or even just a random moment you haven't thought of for some time. Practice recalling it in as much detail as you can muster. You will probably be surprised by the vividness that is available.

Memory Exercise

TOOLS REQUIRED

Just a little peace and quiet

Pencil and paper can be helpful for some people (but not necessary)

So can bus, plane, and car windows

TIME REQUIRED

Can be done in just a few minutes, although longer will provide better results.

RESULT

A treasure trove of memories that you forgot you had access to and a stronger memory.

Meditating on what to write for this essay, I almost decided to delete the whole thing. What good is memory? Why should we strive to remember? Isn't memory inherently sad? When we remember happy memories, we are sad that they are over and now just memories. And when we remember sad memories, well, they are just sad. What good is memory?

Memory Exercise

And yet nostalgia is so seductive, pleasant, and bittersweet. Memory helps you live well. If we are the sum total of our actions—that which we do—then memory reminds us who we are. Remembering our failures teaches us to be humble, and we learn not to repeat our past mistakes. Remembering our triumphs inspires us to be proud of our achievements and to strive for further success. Therefore, memory is a teacher and a guide. It is by memory that we experience the fullness of life, not just the present day, and one's life can be richer for it. It is a way of viewing one's own life as something aesthetically beautiful, replete with meaning, potentially a work of art.

The masters of remembering are memoirists: people who write down their life story so that anyone can experience the story of that person's life. Proust is the most famous example; his book *In Search of Lost Time* is a heroic remembering of his whole life that wells up within him after he eats a cookie, and this sparks the memory of eating the same kind of cookie as a small child. Memories are hidden in objects. A more modern version of the same thing occurs in Karl Ove Knausgaard's gigantic book *My Struggle*. As an adult, he sees a face in the wood grain of his floor, an example of pareidolia (when something that is actually random is perceived as containing a specific image), and it sparks the memory of seeing a face appear in the ocean when he was a small child. From there he begins to remember his whole childhood and then his whole life. Both of these writers of memories show the power of a memory triggered from some small thing that blooms with all of the powerful emotions and experiences of long ago. Anyone can do this. All of us carry the entirety of our whole experience within us at all times. We just forget.

As someone who is not gifted with a very strong memory, I was happy to discover the talents of remembering can be strengthened through practice. It is as simple as doing calisthenics or push-ups for fifteen minutes each morning; except instead of sweating, you sit quietly and recollect.

Take time to recall, in as much detail as possible, memories from your lifetime. Start with your childhood, perhaps your oldest memory, and proceed from there.

After a few run-throughs of this exercise, you may be surprised at what you are able to recall. Strengthening memory in effect strengthens our concept of self. Some of our best ideas and insights may pass us by if we don't take the time to remember the past. We often end up starting from scratch each day, when we should be continuing an ongoing story: the story of a lifetime, not just a day.

If you have trouble remembering, start with a place. Often it is surprisingly easy to remember the structure of places, buildings, and rooms, and from there more details emerge. Remembering can also be aided by thinking of a particular person or by looking at old photographs.

Of course one of the simplest ways to always have ready access to memory is to keep a journal. Listening to music that you used to listen to is also very helpful. In the film *High Fidelity*, John Cusack's character, a record store owner and vinylphile, does not organize his records alphabetically or by genre but "autobiographically"—in the order he first listened to them. As he explains: "If I wanna find the song 'Landslide' by Fleetwood Mac, I have to remember that I bought it for someone in the fall of 1983 pile, but didn't give it to them for personal reasons." For him, every act of listening to music is a chance to be flooded by the memories and feelings associated with a particular day or period of life.

I could tell you that the point of exercising your memory is that it can help you with creativity (it can) and can give you ideas (it will) and allow you to find connections and meaning in things you otherwise would miss (it does), but that is not the point. The point is that memory allows one to appreciate the beauty of life in its entirety, its shape. Every human is the artist of his or her own life. Your life as you have lived it is your greatest work of art, and it is by memory that this art is perceived, is known, is appreciated. The point of memory exercise is to relish the whole tapestry of one's life.

As I write these notes, I take a drink from a glass with ice in it; through the bottom of the glass I can see a light shining, and suddenly a memory wells up inside of me of being a small boy and swimming to the bottom of a swimming pool at night, seeing a light shining at the bottom of the pool. I am there. Every moment, everything I have ever experienced is still present within me, and always will be; it takes only a moment of allowing a light, a scent, a melody, a fragment, or a cookie to summon the experience back. You can look at anything around you and think, What does this remind me of? Memory begins with a question.

Memory is in us, but it is also in things, objects, images, and sights that open up for us. In this way everything we see is filled with life, is filled with potential memories of the life we have already lived, and in this way one can, and should, experience life not just as a day-to-day affair, not just as a present moment, but as an ever piling up accumulation of meaning, of emotion, of life. Memory gives life meaning.

29

Floating in Inner Space

*Our whole culture is about becoming—you gotta get to the
next level, "I got to get the degree, I got to get the house. . . ."
Well, good luck with that, 'cause it's just made up anyway!
The only time you're truly happy is when you're just being.*

—Christopher Messer, floatation tank guru

TECHNIQUE

Lose all sense of the external world by floating in warm saltwater.
By turning off all sources of input from gravity, light, touch, and
sound, you initiate a journey into your own awareness.

D.I.Y. Magic

TOOLS REQUIRED

You actually need a bit of gear for this one, specifically, a floatation tank (see the websites given later in this chapter for locations)

TIME REQUIRED

1 to 2 hours

RESULT

You have to try it to believe it. At the very least it makes you really, really relaxed. At the most it has been claimed to be a shortcut to mindfulness, peace, and brilliant understanding, even enlightenment.

Most of the known techniques for altering and focusing human consciousness/awareness are thousands of years old. It is exceedingly rare that a new tool is discovered. When one is, it takes a while for people to figure out how to use it. Perhaps the floatation tank is such a tool, and its true purpose and importance is yet to be realized.

John C. Lilly pioneered the floatation tank in 1954. The idea is simple. You lie down in a dark tub of warm water loaded with

enough salt so that you just float there. With the body no longer sending sensory signals of any kind to the brain, the mind is freed to turn inward. This revolutionary technique has not been widely investigated; not much has come from it, other than the unfortunate 1980 movie *Altered States*. But we should not be too quick to dismiss the floatation tank's potential. The microscope was invented in 1590, but nobody really knew what to do with the darn thing. It was over eighty years before Antonie van Leeuwenhoek thought to use it on organic matter, thus discovering microorganisms and revolutionizing biology and medicine.

Currently, floatation tanks are recommended to achieve perfect states of relaxation, but I suspect they may enable much more. I recommend that if you can track down a nearby tank, you give it a spin.

I first got the chance to try one at Common Ground, a holistic wellness center in Portland. I asked the spa manager at Common Ground, "Who uses the floatation tank and why?" She said, "Some people, mostly young guys, come in expecting to trip out when they try it, but that's not really likely." Her regular users report it's great for a variety of ailments, from back pain to arthritis. She also described it as "training wheels for meditation . . . one and a half hours in the floatation tank [are] equal to five hours of REM sleep." She instructed me to be careful not to get any of the saltwater in my eyes and to fully relax and let the water support my weight.

I also spoke with Christopher Messer, a founder of Float On, a floatation tank shop in Portland, who compared floating to meditation: "This is the same thing the Buddhist monks are trying to do. But this is it without falling asleep and getting the rap on the shoulder with a stick. When there is no external stimulation, the internal mind has to take over. Thought goes away, identity goes away. It's about effortless doing."

When I first entered the tank, the sensation of floating on my back effortlessly in the warm water was so startling that it was impossible to resist the temptation to play and wiggle around like a fish, enjoying the new sense of buoyancy. The saltwater makes floating as easy as lying down on the couch. With eight hundred pounds of salt, the water keeps your arms, legs, and torso floating up out of the water, which is shockingly only ten inches deep! Even my head, when fully relaxed, was supported upright enough so that I didn't have to worry about water getting in my eyes or nose. After splashing around for a bit, I quieted down and settled into the experience.

I began to get the uncanny feeling that I was spinning, as though my head were suddenly veering off to the left or the right, like my whole body was beginning to whirl around. It wasn't a violent sensation at all, but more like a gentle suggestion that seemed to fade when I paid attention to it. From time to time I would bob up against one of the sides of the tank and then, with a gentle push, float off in the other direction very slowly. I was wearing earplugs to keep the water out, and it helped with sound reduction. It was pitch dark, which I have always found, interestingly, to be not black but a very dark gray—the brain gray, or *eigengrau*, that is still perceived by the brain even in total absence of light.

The idea behind all of this is that your body isn't taking in any sensory information; that attention is free to go elsewhere. Think of the analogy of an overloaded computer that suddenly has shut down half of its programs; it's bound to run a whole lot more smoothly. (Indeed you might extend that analogy and say that the point of practices such as meditation or floatation is to reboot the hard drive.)

At first the bodily sensation of, well, having a body was greatly increased. Gradually, however, I adapted to the feeling of floating, and my arms, legs, neck, and body seemed to melt away. I have a fleeting memory of the sort of images that linger from a half-forgotten dream: a river, a boat, lights, polar bears? And then I was startled from my trance by soft music indicating that my session was over. An hour and a half had gone by as swiftly as a good night's rest. Had I completely zonked out? If so, I was quite comfortable levitating on a bed of water, but the state seemed to me more akin to the strange trance-like fugue that I experience whenever I get acupuncture. A refreshing, revitalizing state resembling sleep, but one that is more conscious and more aware than sleep.

I left the session with a definite feeling of lightness and nonchalance. In a word—high.

Floatation tanks are still a novelty; they are rare and the costs of owning one are prohibitive for most people. However, if you get the chance, the experience is definitely worth seeking out.* Devotees to floating like Messer, who has owned a tank for years, see floating as the next step in human consciousness: "Our culture is about change from the outside in. But you change it from the inside out and it's going to work. Consciousness just wants to become more consciousness. This is what the tank is doing. There are areas that were once unconscious, and consciousness is saying—I want to be here. Consciousness is expanding itself. And the float tank fits that perfectly. Floating is just a way to get back to your natural state."

---

* For more information, or to see if there is a floatation tank near you, check out floatation.com, floatationlocations.com, and samadhitank.com.

30

Potions, Libations & Herbs

O, mickle is the powerful grace that lies
In plants, herbs, stones, and their true qualities
For naught so vile that on the earth doth live
But to the earth some good doth give.

—William Shakespeare

TECHNIQUE

Don't try everything in this chapter at once! Your brain will short
out. This chapter is a fecund cornucopia, nay, a veritable frothing
cauldron of quaffable libations. Just dog-ear a couple recipes to try
for now. Come back for the rest later.

TOOLS REQUIRED

A healthy constitution—this sort of experimentation is not for
    everybody. Know your limits.

Betel nut

Coffee

Yerba maté

Naps

Whiskey

Kava

Tea

Butter tea

Chia seeds

Abstinence

Nootropics

Poetry

Vitamins

TIME REQUIRED

A few months, if you space these experiments out a bit, which is
recommended.

RESULT

The human experience can be tweaked, juiced, goosed, filtered, smoothed, enhanced, and recalibrated a dozen ways, as needed, with stuff that's mostly available at the supermarket. Find out what works for you.

No grimoire would be complete without a section detailing the various herbs, recipes, and potions available to those seeking to modify their reality. I will skip the standard drugs such as pot, mushrooms, and LSD, not because they don't belong here but because volumes have already been written on those subjects. We will focus instead on drugs of a more subtle, but also perhaps less familiar, variety.

Please note: Before trying any mind-altering substances, be aware of your body's limits.

PAAN OR BETEL NUT

What it is and where to get it: Paan, consisting of betel leaf, areca nut, and lime paste, all chewed together is the drug of choice for most cabbies in India (as well as in Pakistan, the Philippines, Vietnam, and Bangladesh). It is available at some small Asian markets

(usually in the freezer section). All three ingredients—the paste, the nut, and the leaf—must be used in conjunction. You should be able to procure enough of all three to host a backyard betel party for about five bucks.

How to take it: Cut a bit of the green nut off and dice it up. It's very tough. Spread a smidgen of the slaked lime paste on the leaf and then wrap it around the chopped areca nut like you're folding up a piece of dolma. Pop it inside your cheek and periodically give it a couple of chomps, like a cow chewing her cud. It will quickly begin to produce voluminous amounts of bright orange saliva. Spit, don't swallow.

The amount of drooling and spitting necessary while chewing betel is quite hilarious. It has a pleasing anesthetic effect on the mouth. And you will quickly feel a lightness in the skull and cheekbones, a brightness in the eyes, and a desire for conversation and strolling. Because it is conducive to conversation, this is a great drug to try with a friend. The eagerness to talk is somewhat mitigated by the amazing buckets of bright orange frothy saliva that the drug stimulates. Is it any wonder this drug never caught on in the West, where we are overobsessed with appearances? Sadly, drooling in public is considered crude in our society.

The payoff: A mild euphoria that is blended with a scintillating clarity, much like the feeling experienced by watching a really good film: It makes you feel like conversing with a friend and

maybe taking a walk—magical yet subtle. In many cultures it is seen as a prerequisite to meaningful and friendly conversation.

WAY TOO MUCH COFFEE

What it is and where to get it: When coffee first became popular in the Ottoman Empire and the sultan heard that the common people were drinking a black wine that made them smarter instead of dumber, he outlawed it immediately, fearing it could sow the seeds of rebellion. Can coffee be a revolutionary beverage? It depends on how strong you make it. Personally I prefer to buy good-quality whole beans and grind them myself at home. I recommend using the kind of grinder you power by hand; few things are more annoying than the sound of an electric grinder at seven in the morning. Of course coffee shops are great too, but the quality can vary a lot from place to place.

How to take it: Your coffee should be freshly ground and brewed strong, and you should drink a lot of it. If you are drinking quality beans, there is no need for cream or sugar; coffee tastes good black if it is good-quality coffee. It is fine if you do add these things, but they shouldn't be necessary. Caffeinated consciousness is a state of mind that can be quite different depending on whether you are alone or with others. Experienced by yourself it can be the most productive thing in the world. On the other hand, I have seen a group of four or five people each down four or five cups of strong black joe and the conversation devolved into chirping squirrel-like noises. Delightful.

The payoff: It is easy to underestimate the power of coffee because we are so used to it. However, drinking a badass ton of coffee (three-plus cups of the strong stuff) can produce a remarkable state of mind that is as peculiar and reality-bending as many other more vaunted drugs.

YERBA MATÉ

What it is and where to get it: Yerba maté is no doubt a lot healthier and less addictive than many of the other substances mentioned so far. A five-pound bag of loose-leaf yerba maté can be found at stores that specialize in South American items for like $5. That's a lot of yerba maté, but you will need it. The trick here is to brew it ridiculously strong. The premade swill they sell in cans at the supermarket is a useless scam, like soaking used coffee filters in cold water and calling it coffee.

How to take it: Yerba maté must be made fresh and sipped continuously throughout the day. The proper way to imbibe is to drink maté out of a gourd with a little metal *bombilla* straw. In a pinch, you can brew it up in a French press and then serve it chilled and cut with lemonade. Maté lemonade is the very best drink in the world to enjoy while playing chess.

The payoff: At first glance, one might think this instills simply a caffeinated consciousness akin to coffee or tea. This probably just means you aren't drinking enough of it. When you hit the plateau of buzz, it vibrates at a higher frequency than caffeine. A chemical compound called mateine is responsible for the jolt of energy, one that can give you all of the energy and momentum provided by a cup of espresso or coffee, but with a clean burn: There are none of the coffee jitters or anxieties associated with coffee. Another bonus is that it doesn't seem to disrupt sleep patterns like coffee does.

NAPS

What it is and where to get it: Far be it from me to tell anyone how to nap. You can nap on a couch, in a hammock, in a patch of sunshine, or curled up on a rainy day. Take as needed.

How to take it: There is a lot of debate about when the ideal time for a nap is. Although this question may never be fully answered, the widely accepted theory is ideal napping happens around two o'clock, and in more tropical climates, whenever the heat of the sun is hottest. However, there are many renegade schools of thought that advocate for sneaking in a midmorning catnap, and even some who favor the early evening beauty rest. Feel free to experiment. You can nap in ten-minute increments or take a luxurious two-hour snooze.

The payoff: The effects are potent, rejuvenating, and immediate. A well-timed nap can provide a fresh take on the day; it can

refresh the mind, reset the mood, revitalize the spirit, and refuel the body. An often overlooked and yet powerful stimulant and visionary state!

WRITING WHISKEY

What it is and where to get it: Whiskey is a great elixir for writing. Naturally the place to find it is in bars, but bars are generally not conducive to great writing because invariably someone comes along and asks, "What you are writing?" and before you know it, you are *talking* about your book instead of *writing* it. Writing whiskey is therefore best consumed alone, at home, which is part of why it is a dangerous practice!

How to take it: Many writers have their own signature drink. William Faulkner had the mint julep, Ernest Hemingway preferred the mojito, Carson McCullers was fueled by a thermos of hot tea and sherry that she named "Sonnie Boy," Dorothy Parker was a fan of the whiskey sour, and Charles Bukowski drank whatever he could get his hands on. You can concoct your own signature libation or steal one from the greats. It is fun to invent your own: I have come up with a concoction that is one part bourbon to two parts tart cherry juice. I call it the Sundowner and enjoy it at the end of a good day of writing or when I want to get a few extra pages done in the evening.

The payoff: A sufficient supply should be able to turn anybody with half a soul into a prolific writer. Obviously this can be a dangerous technique! Use with care. The list of great writers who used this trick is long. Of course, their lives might have been longer too, if they had gone easier on their livers.

KAVA

What it is and where to get it: The kava plant has an effect that is all its own. It is made from the ground-up kava root indigenous to Polynesia. Kava is a great way to relax without alcohol; it is mostly a body high. It bestows a pleasantly mellow feeling, one that, unlike alcohol, leaves the mind completely lucid but languid. You can still think clearly, and it won't impair your ability to drive a car, but why drive anywhere when you would much rather chill in a hammock? A couple bowls of this stuff and you feel like you are on island time. It can be hard to find here on the mainland, but there are a few Internet resources you can order it from.

How to take it: The preparation of kava is part of the fun; you take the finely ground kava root and put it in a cloth bag and squish it around in a large bowl of water until you have a nice earthy bowl of kava. This takes a while. You can also go the more modern route of mixing it in a blender and then pouring it through a strainer. While some might disagree with using such modern technology, when you consider that the three-thousand-year-old traditional method involved the female virgins of the tribe chewing up the kava root and spitting it out into a communal basin, modern technology starts to look pretty appealing.

The payoff: It kind of looks and tastes like an earthy mud puddle, and I mean that in a good way. As soon as you drink a mouthful, your tongue begins to numb; with a few more bowls, that feeling spreads to your stomach and limbs, imparting a mellow, muscle-soothing feeling that is incredibly relaxing. Best enjoyed with friends.

TEA

What it is and where to get it: Tea often loses out to coffee, thanks to the latter's reputation as the more powerful stimulant. This could be because we don't make a proper cuppa tea like the British and God intended. The British empire (1583–1945) was built on pots of tea with exceedingly strong character. Tea is available everywhere, but good tea takes a little extra attention and time to be made well.

How to take it: While tea bags are fine in a hurry, once you go to loose-leaf tea you have more control over how strong you want to make your tea, and there are thousands more varieties to choose, from five-hundred-mile chai, so named because Indian truck drivers ask the chai wallah for a cup strong enough to drive another five hundred miles, to the more Zen-like quality of a cup of Japanese green tea. George Orwell has this to say about tea:

Tea should be strong. For a pot holding a quart, if you are going to fill it nearly to the brim, six heaped teaspoons would be about right. I maintain that one strong cup of tea is better than twenty weak ones. All true tea lovers not only like their tea strong, but like it a little stronger with each year that passes.

The rest of Orwell's recipe insists that tea is spoiled with sugar, although cream is OK, and that it is very important to warm up the pot beforehand. Also, the water should still be boiling upon impact with the leaves.

The payoff: While I do appreciate Orwell's conviction, I don't think there is just one right way to make tea; there are thousands of varieties of tea from cultures all over the globe. The point is that tea is something to be taken seriously, and when made well and with attention to detail it is a force to be reckoned with. Indeed, when compared with the more standard morning cup of coffee, drinking tea is an alternate way of life.

YAK BUTTER TEA

What it is and where to get it: Confession: I haven't actually tried making yak butter tea using real yak butter at home. While it is possible to order yak butter online, I recommend simply using grass-fed cow butter as a replacement. That way this recipe can be an everyday option. If you're vegan, you can make it with coconut oil. I got turned on to butter tea after frequenting a Tibetan restaurant; the tea was perfect for warming up on cold winter days. Drinking hot tea with butter, yak or not, is actually a quite different experience from just drinking tea, because it really does impart a huge surge of energy! The energy boost seems to come from all the nutritious fats in the butter. The caffeine doesn't hurt either.

How to take it: Yak butter tea (and its alternatives) is great for battling the winter blues. You brew a strong pot of black tea (loose-leaf pu-erh tea is the best; as an added bonus, this tea is believed to be a panacea for everything from hangovers to weight loss), and then pour it in a blender along with a big splash of cream, a heaping tablespoon of butter, and a large pinch of salt. Blend until it's frothy, and drink immediately. It is an acquired taste, and to be honest, some people can't stand the stuff! It has a strange and gamey flavor. I recommend using only top-notch, grass-fed organic butter for this. Drink it hot.

The payoff: This is the national beverage of Tibet; it's a comforting and energizing drink that is great for cold weather, high altitudes, and strenuous work. There is a currently popular variation of this that swaps out the pu-erh tea for coffee, but I feel like it is best to stick to the original recipe.

ISKIATE OR CHIA FRESCA

What it is and where to get it: Iskiate, also known as chia fresca, is pretty much a Paleolithic version of Red Bull. You can buy the seeds nowadays in just about any health-food store. They come in a big pouch that will generally last a long time.

How to take it: I like to drink this at the start of the day when I know I am going to need some extra energy. Iskiate is the ultimate pre-workout drink. Mix together a couple heaping spoonfuls of chia seeds with lots of sugar and lime juice in a glass of water. Let this sit for a few minutes. It gels into a weird crunchy goop that resembles frog eggs, but it tastes much better than it looks! It has a nice nutty flavor that becomes addictive.

The payoff: This is the energy drink of the Tarahumara Indians, a tribe of world-class ultrarunners who power their ultramarathon-length runs through the canyons of the Mexican barranca with this drink.

Recently I have seen chia drinks pop up in cans in supermarkets. Steer clear of that and make your own.

EVEN MORE OPTIONS

Abstinence

No, not absinthe, abstinence; that's right! Abstinence can be mind-altering in the context of whatever stimulants your brain is used to; by altering the flow of caffeine, sex, alcohol, or whatever you're using, you are changing the chemical cocktail in your brain. Let's say, for example, you're a bit of a barfly. This weekend go to the most packed bar you can find and stay there until closing while sipping only a soft drink. The result will be eye-opening.

I have had more than one friend claim that the raging psychosis and temporary mental impairment brought on by quitting nicotine cold turkey is something so surreal it can be enjoyed, like free drugs. I also know a guy whose life underwent radical transformations after he gave up masturbation for a few months! (He got married.) Boxers have been known to forgo sex for weeks leading up to a big match. The chemistry of withdrawal is powerful. Whether any experience is enjoyable or just plain sucks depends on how you frame it.

Nootropics

Nootropics encompass a very wide and loosely defined category of substances that are designed to give a person greater mental focus and energy. In the future, I expect that research into these areas will figure out exactly what supplements are helpful for focusing the human brain. For now, you can find them in the health supplement section of your local organic grocery store. Vitamins, ginkgo biloba, Bacopa, royal jelly—the list is too long to fully catalog here, and more research needs to be done before we truly know what is effective. There are also currently a few all-in-one "smart drugs" on the market, and I have experienced noticeable results from trying Alpha BRAIN in particular. Not only did they give me an edge to my chess game, they actually can cure the common hangover, I kid you not!

Too Much Poetry

Those who don't realize you can be totally wasted on words have simply not consumed enough poetry in one sitting. Most people haven't, in my experience. People who read just one or two poems and then see no point in poetry are like people who have tried one or two sips of wine and don't understand intoxication. Furthermore, they say they don't like the taste because they have undeveloped palates. Philistines!

In order to understand poetry you must become intoxicated. Go on a binge. Read for hours, read out loud until you stumble outside and the world is bright and rippling with new layers of meaning shot through with light. If the poet you're reading can't do this for you, find another poet.

Dream Steroids: Valerian + Vitamin B6 + Melatonin

Valerian, vitamin B6, and melatonin are all available at your local health-food store for a few bucks per bottle. Any one of them will enhance the depth and vividness of your dreams. Taken together they are a powerful cocktail ensured to give you access to some of the most powerful and memorable dreams you will ever have. Not bad for $20.

I am sure there is plenty of stuff I left off this list, but you get the idea. Even more than producing an endless list of legal drugs, the point is that our definition of what is and isn't a drug is amorphous and can and should be questioned and challenged. In this way we begin to see just how malleable our reality truly is, for such slight alterations to our physical state can have huge effects on our mental state, which of course affects our experience of reality itself. Life is an experience that can be played with endlessly, and we should learn how to play in every register and octave of our instrument possible, and not just stay in the one spot that is thought of as normal.

31

Fasting

There's a hidden sweetness in the stomach's emptiness.
We are lutes, no more, no less. If the soundbox
is stuffed full of anything, no music.
If the brain and the belly are burning clean
with fasting, every moment a new song comes out of the fire.
The fog clears, and new energy makes you
run up the steps in front of you.

—Jalal āl-Din Rumī

TECHNIQUE

Don't eat any food for one day. Choosing to not eat for a whole day
has been used for health, for spirituality, for focus; how you choose
to use it is up to you.

TOOLS REQUIRED

Plenty of water

Some recommend having juice, lemon water, or broth; that's fine
but not necessary

TIME REQUIRED

1 day

RESULT

A self-made holiday

A day set apart

A new understanding of food

A tried-and-true method for turning away from day-to-day concerns and facing the interior, fasting clears and focuses the mind. It has a long history as an integral part of many cultures and most religions. In the Eastern Orthodox religion, it is tied to the principle of the body (*soma*) and the soul (*pneuma*) being two halves of the same whole. Whatever happens to one affects the other, and with fasting you strengthen and clean out both. In the Hindu re-

ligion, it is often customary to fast on different days, depending on one's sect: every Monday for devotees of Shiva, Thursdays for devotees of Vishnu, and so on. (In this case, the fast usually occurs from sunrise to sunset, and a meal is eaten at the beginning of the day.) The Koran states that through fasting one gains *taqwa*, or God consciousness. Ultimately, fasting is too simple to need explanation and can, simply, only be experienced.

Schedule when you're going to try this experiment at least a week in advance; you will want a day when you're not doing anything too strenuous or stressful. It is a day for introspection and contemplation. Also, the day before a fast, you don't want to pig out on burgers and fries or the like because then your body will just be processing the food from the day before. Always drink plenty of water. You should fast only if you are in good health, and I recommend a fast of one day as being plenty for most people. Before you embark on your fast, talk with your doctor to determine if you have any health issues or reasons why fasting may not be right for you. As with everything in this book, please use common sense and don't overdo it. This is not a diet plan or a way to try to lose weight! But fasting for one day, once in a while, is medically safe as long as you are careful.

32

Beards & Other Transformations

There is much to support the view that it is our clothes that wear us, and not the other way around.

—Virginia Woolf

TECHNIQUE

Change the way you look to change the way others see you, to change the way you see yourself in others' eyes, to change the way you see yourself, and to change the way you are.

TOOLS REQUIRED (PICK ONE)

A beard
Sunglasses
A disguise

A fake accent

A Hawaiian shirt, or other clothing you wouldn't normally wear

If you already have an accent, a beard, a Hawaiian shirt, and sunglasses, then do something different, obviously. Also, congratulations!

TIME REQUIRED

As long as you like

RESULT

Trick the world into thinking you are someone different, and suddenly you will find yourself in a different world.

⚜

Being a full-grown man, I take advantage of the power nature has given me to grow my own fully fuzzy, woolly, organic neck scarf and face muffler every winter. In other words, I grow a big, bushy beard. It's really quite the robust specimen too, because it doesn't just grow downward like most people's facial hair, but actually seems to jut outward like a furry cactus, giving me a resemblance somewhat akin to Bluto from Popeye, further enhanced by a shock

of white on my chin that occurred when a friend of mine passed away some years ago. I shave it all off in the summertime because it gets hot and itchy, but in my opinion every guy who is able should grow a full beard in the winter, and then trim it when the days grow long, like the seasonal change of a tree's foliage. If you are a male who lives above the fifty-fourth parallel, and you don't rock a beard in the wintertime, you really must ask yourself why.

The answer, of course, is one sad word: *fashion*. Men shave because that is what is expected. I proffer the argument that someday, in the future, when we are a more enlightened species, all men will unabashedly grow a thick and luxurious beard in the wintertime. Yes, someday the practice of shaving will be viewed with the same incredulous contempt that we now feel when contemplating such backward practices as wearing white powdered wigs or corsets and bustles. That is all just a friendly piece of my mind, but here is where I'm going with this (and my apologies to the lady readers who just waded through that diatribe): When you wear a beard, people treat you differently. It is minor but definite. A beard, or the lack of one, creates a small but perceptible, very real, and palpable shift in the weave of reality that you inhabit.

You walk into, say, the exact same coffee shop with a beard and people treat you with a little bit more reserve than they do if you have none. It almost adds a slight invisibility cloaking effect. It is, to be sure, a subtle effect—less like the invisibility granted by

Harry Potter's cloak, and more like Obi-Wan Kenobi's "These aren't the droids you're looking for."

This is just one example of the sort of appearance hacking that represents a basic and easy cantrip anybody can practice anywhere. The reasons behind the change are fairly complex. For one thing, I think when you are clean-shaven, people can read your face more easily, and so you seem more open and approachable. Also, shaving is a form of emasculation. It makes you appear more androgynous, whereas a beard suggests a bit of the Wildman; beards are for lumberjacks, hobos, hippies, and Walt Whitman. My point is simply that this is a very noticeable example of how you can be treated differently, instantly, based on appearance. In other words (and to anyone who gives a damn about fashion I suppose this is old news), when we meet people, the first thing we meet isn't *them*, it is the visual *appearance of them*. Of course this encapsulates a lot more than appearance but also demeanor, timbre of voice, emotional affect, and so on.

I don't want to go on and on about fashion, which means many different things to different people, but I will say that to the magus, fashion can also become a means to an end. Appearances make all the difference on first meeting someone. The obvious takeaway here is one should dress nicely and make a good impression; that's a truism that everybody and their grandmother has heard before. But the magus is one who takes this simple concept and is able to hack it and use it to his or her own ends. You can become an entirely different person by costume.

Beards & Other Transformations

There is a subtle difference here between what I'm talking about and the usual definition of a disguise. A disguise is *in order to fool others* by presenting a false identity to the world. This idea is that you change your appearance to the world *in order to fool yourself.* On some days, the magus may want to take center stage and use charisma and modes of dress to appear as some sort of rock star, icon, or hero, but on other days the magus may want to disappear into the anonymity of a baseball cap and a nondescript jacket; she is equally adept at using clothes as a cloak to appear in the guise of a businessperson or as a hobo. The magus is able to appear to the world as however she wishes, because the magus realizes this basic precept underpinning human sociology and uses it to her own ends. It is really the same thing that teenagers are doing each day by experimenting with their wardrobes and presenting a persona to the world. However, I'm proposing a conscious hacking of this idea.

This sort of self-transformation is not about fitting in, it's about reforming the way reality fits you; use it to your own nefarious or benevolent ends. One easy exercise is to make sketches of yourself in bizarre outfits. Try to picture yourself dressed in a way that is really unusual for you, whether that is as a jock, or hippie, or steampunk, or whatever you like; just make it an unusual mode compared to what you're accustomed to. (How much of day-to-day reality is simply habit anyways?) If you don't usually wear a fedora, then give it a try, but if you already do, then see what happens when you don a Boston Red Sox cap instead. Then actually play the part. Get out of your comfort zone.

You're not your clothes, but a lot of people don't know that. See what it feels like to dress like a person you would see on the street as a stranger and not understand. You can try this for $40 or less. Try shopping at a thrift store and buy a costume. Dress up in your new duds and go walk around. Go grocery shopping or hang out at a café, make a point of talking to some strangers while in your "disguise," and you will be shocked at how much of an effect this actually has on how people respond to you.

All of this is just a faster way of growing a beard, so to speak. It is a method for toying with the fabric of society that we swim in every day and so remain blind to because of its ubiquity, like the fish in the parable who are unable to grasp the concept of water.*

Part of this basic spell's power lies in how it allows us to see that the way people see us affects how they treat us, which in return affects how we behave, creating a feedback loop of sorts that is much more modifiable than we might realize. How much of our own personal concept of self is based on what we read in the mirror of other people's eyes?

---

* Two young fish are swimming along together at the bottom of the sea. They pass an old-timer fish who greets them with, "How's the water?" They nod and swim on by. After a while one of the young fish turns to the other and asks, "What the hell is water?"

33

Trance & Reverie

I was trying to daydream, but my mind kept wandering.
—Steven Wright

TECHNIQUE

Listen to the way the rain makes you feel, the way the world appears in early morning fog, and at sunset and sunrise, the way the light slants through the trees; notice the unnoticed. Find yourself lost in reverie.

TOOLS REQUIRED

An eye for shadows
Candle, moon, and firelight

Journeys by water
Other quiet and strange places and moments

TIME REQUIRED

Just enough time to lose track of time

RESULT

Access to the inner world.

※

We typically switch through many varying levels of consciousness, even during a single day. Compare the mental state of focus you are experiencing right now, while reading, to other times of the day when you are walking about, exercising, watching TV, day-dreaming, sleeping, working, grocery shopping, cooking, driving, surfing the Internet, or talking with friends. The aperture of focus within your own mind necessary to perform each of these actions dilates considerably from one activity to the next. While some involve total engagement, other activities can be performed without much conscious thought—when the body goes on autopilot and the mind is somewhere else, you enter a trance or reverie.

Trance, reverie, and other altered states of consciousness are

every bit as valid as everyday "normal" consciousness/reality, and we inhabit them much more often than we realize. Most people are quite familiar with the self-induced trance known as highway hypnosis, aka "white line fever"; after driving a long distance on a highway, we find on arriving that we had slipped into a waking trance, and the past hours have disappeared in seemingly no time at all. This is because we are able to drive on autopilot; the conscious, self-aware mind is free to drift away from the mundane physical world. The same thing happens when we fall into a reverie while staring at the rippling waves of a lake, or flickering logs on a fire.

If you take practices from across countless fields, cultures, religions, modes of being, and systems of ritual (hypnosis, song and dance, duende, speaking in tongues, enchantment, faith healing, divination, out-of-body experience, sweat lodges, drumming, yoga, drugs, fever, and on and on), you'll find we are really talking about the same thing: a state in which the mind lets go of the normal way of being and is opened up to an experience of existence as a whole that is bigger and without time. This state can be considered liminal: a place between two worlds, a state of mind in which one occupies both the external and the internal worlds.

For our purposes we will define this liminal state as *trance* when it is reached through a process of repetition, like drumming, dance, or running, and as *reverie* when it is slipped into almost by accident, while staring at a campfire or gazing out of a moving window at a blurred landscape. Trance and reverie are two different ways to approach the liminal.

For trances, the trick lies in the repetition; we become oblivious to anything that becomes so second nature we do it without thinking and can become lost in the rhythm, the loop, the moment, the movement. To put it another way, in trance we become blind to the world, the world of surface, objects, nouns, things; these all become a blur. We enter into a state of pure being.

Slipping into a reverie is easier to try than trance, simply because you don't have to learn a special skill like drumming to try it; you just have to find something beautiful to stare at. Different people will find that different activities work for them. Staring at a campfire is one of my favorites, but long walks can be equally hypnotic.

Rather than spell out the hundred and one different ways you can use trance or reverie to approach the liminal, I think it is enough to be aware of the similarities and allow yourself to slip into that state of mind when the opportunity presents itself.

Sure, you can go looking for it, but these windows into our inner selves present themselves so frequently, the best method is just to cultivate an awareness of them and allow yourself to go deeper when the chance arises. Imagine what a culture change that would be! What if it were more common to see someone enjoying a trance or a reverie in public than to see people zoned out on the digital window of their phones?

Often the approach to the liminal has a way of sneaking up on us when we least expect it; the best practice is to simply be ready for it! If life is a tapestry or an image, then picture the reverse side of this tapestry; the design and figures become abstract and less clear, and yet it is this hidden side of things that holds everything together and shows how the whole coheres.

34

Neuro-Linguistic Literature & Programming

Reading is the sole means by which we slip, involuntarily, often helplessly, into another's skin, another's voice, another's soul.

—Joyce Carol Oates

TECHNIQUE

Pay attention to the mental diet you eat every day. Consciously decide what diet you're going to consume with your reading. Just like food nutrition for the physical body, with your mental existence, you are what you read.

D.I.Y. Magic

TOOLS REQUIRED

Good books
Even better, great books
Check out the bibliography on page 250 for starters

TIME REQUIRED

At least a hundred pages

RESULT

A mental headspace that is clean, healthy, and ready to do any
heavy lifting.

It is strange, but aside from the highly academic, the biggest
students of how language affects the structure and perception of
reality—known as neuro-linguistic programing (NLP)—often
seem to be pickup artists and car salesmen! Yet, the magus is one
who finds new uses and applications for otherwise forgotten,
obscure, and unusual ideas, so let us now consider the power of
language.

Just as we are shaped by the place we live in and the friends

we talk to, we are shaped by the language we hear, read, and think. The idea behind this spell is that the very language, and the words that we choose to use, convey much more meaning than is apparent on the surface.

One way to become cognizant of this reality is to steep yourself in the language of a particular author. Upon reading some work of literature, in a large quantity, rapidly in one sitting, the observant reader will notice that immediately after, their world, their perceptions, have been colored by the ideas of the author they were just reading. Upon closing *Swann's Way* or *Crime and Punishment* or *The Catcher in the Rye*, we find that the world we inhabit is a Proustian or a Dostoyevskian one; we become a bit more like Holden Caulfield than we already were. The student of magic and literature should therefore learn how to imbue his life with the hues of his own choosing, as he likes.

Language, Logos, is how we construct our human world. It is thought. Naturally then, any large amounts of carefully wrought language that we input into our own stream of conscious will influence the course and the outcome of our thoughts.

Try this: Pick a novel, preferably a classic, because they've got what it takes as far as the caliber of the prose goes. And read it in one day if you can. If not, then in as few days as possible. Observe how you are able to inhabit the world of that writer by steeping yourself in language.

35

A Vision Quest

Ideas are fishes. If you want to catch a little fish you can stay in the shallow water. But if you want to catch the big fish you've got to go deeper.

—David Lynch

TECHNIQUE

Spend time in the wild to let your mind open up, to think. Go out into nature, and find a good spot to just wait and see what happens when you sit quietly in a beautiful place that you feel some connection to.

D.I.Y. Magic

TOOLS REQUIRED

Woods are preferable; a mountaintop or anywhere with wildlife
    and solitude
Patience
Hiking boots, clothes, water, and food for the day
A notebook (optional)

TIME REQUIRED

1 day (or longer, as needed)

RESULTS

Find the perfect fishing spot for catching new ideas, insights, and
revelations.

⚜

In a *New York Times* interview, the musician Joanna Newsom
described the time she was a teenager and went on a vision quest—
a period of quiet reflection, alone in nature, rooted to one spot.[*]

---

[*] See Jody Rosen, "Joanna Newsom, the Changeling," *New York Times*, March 3, 2010.

Newsom spent days camping alone by a riverside. "On the third day, I was kind of delirious. I'd only eaten a little rice. I'd just slept and looked at a river for three days. I was prepared to be visited by my spirit animal—I was just sitting there, saying some sort of prayer, inviting that presence into my life." She saw this experience as transformative: "I was a completely different person before I went to the river, and a completely different person after."[*]

Nowadays this is an unusual thing for an eighteen-year-old to do, but throughout the majority of human history, people have gone on vision quests. Young people used to go on vision quests to mark the transition from childhood to adulthood, while people at life crossroads needing guidance and direction would do the same. And while a vision quest is something more specific than just a walk in the woods, it's worth noting that time spent in nature has inspired countless great thinkers, from writers like Thoreau and Edward Abbey to numerous other artists, creators, and scientists.

A return to the quiet and stillness of nature can recharge your batteries, and when you are truly away from it all, you can get a handle on things from a new perspective.

Go spend time by yourself in nature. Wherever you go, you should be and feel alone. Choose somewhere peaceful, a creek side, meadow, or hilltop, and wait; listen to the sounds around you, feel

---

* See Erik Davis, "Nearer the Heart of Things," *Arthur*, no. 25 (winter 2006).

the stillness and the freshness of the air, and linger . . . until you have a realization, a revelation, a big idea. Not just a regular idea, but the kind you have to write down or draw. The kind where you slap your forehead in shock. Wait there as long as it takes.

The point of this exercise is that often we think that problem solving or creativity has to be something that we do, that we make happen. But when you take the time to go out into nature and just be there, you will see that big ideas have a way of coming along when we are doing nothing more than quietly paying attention.

36

Memory Palaces
& Mental Golems,
or
the New Art of Daemonology

This Daemon of Socrates was not an apparition, but rather a sensible perception of a voice, or an apprehension of some words, which after an unaccountable manner affected him; as in a dream there is no real voice, yet we have fancies and apprehensions of words which make us imagine that we hear someone speak. —Plutarch, *Morals*, vol. 2

TECHNIQUE

Congrats, you've made it to the end of the book. Since you have just finished a 101 course on magic, here is an advanced spell. Proceed only if you are ready.

Create a make-believe thought form with your imagination and coax it to come to life.

Pick an image, a being. First see it, hold the image in your head until you can picture it clearly. Then practice imagining what it would say if it spoke to you. Gradually this takes on a life of its own.

Warning: Be careful what you create! Don't try this experiment unless you've already tried all the other spells in this book. This is advanced magic.

TOOLS REQUIRED

Your imagination

TIME REQUIRED

Several sessions over the space of a week or two

RESULT

An adviser, a guide, a capricious sprite at your beck and call. And the pleasure of time spent walking around just talking to yourself . . . or are you?

I once read a book about the art of constructing memory palaces: vivid and stable structures existing wholly within the mind. I can't tell you the exact name of the book, because I don't remember. (The experience of not having access to some tidbit of information is an endangered feeling because we now can have immediate and total recall of damn near all recorded information in the world instantaneously via the Internet. Will the power of memory become a weakened, vestigial organ?)

The art of the memory palace, or the method of loci, as it is also known, was well known to the ancient Greeks. If you were a contemporary of Socrates and you wanted ready access to a piece of information, you had to store it in your head. Interestingly, the practice of the method of loci has recently come back into usage in modern memory competitions, where contestants memorize strings of random digits, shuffled cards, and so on. I can't see much point in that. But it was while trying out the method of loci technique

that I stumbled on the discovery of how to create a mental golem, or daemon, in the classic sense of the word. I will explain what I mean by that in a moment, but first it helps to understand what exactly a memory palace is because it seems the mind must first create a suitable and sturdy imagined environment before it can create an entity therein.

It is said Simonides, the fellow who stumbled on the technique for creating memory palaces, realized how to do so after narrowly escaping being crushed by stone pillars that toppled over during an earthquake at a banquet he was attending. You can imagine the scene, a bunch of Greeks lounging about on pillows eating grapes and debating philosophy. The doorbell rings and it's for Simonides; he goes to receive his visitors and as soon as he walks outside into the courtyard, the earthquake strikes and squishes everybody inside along with the grapes. It seems that the remains were so badly flattened that nobody could tell who was who among the dead, which was a problem for families who wanted to be able to bury and eulogize their relatives and not the body of some random stranger. Simonides was able to identify all of the remains by creating a perfect static mental image of the scene and where each person was sitting at the banquet table just before he walked out. From this experience, he realized that one can construct a spatially organized and stable architecture seen only in the mind, and that by holding this blueprint firmly in place, a person can then walk around freely within the memory palace just as though it were a real building.*

It was while constructing my own memory palace that I hit on the technique of creating a mental golem, which I will explain here. A mental golem is what I call an imaginary being who is animated by the unconscious. Think of it as an imaginary friend for grown-ups. My original idea was to create a sort of librarian or guardian of the mental palace: an imaginary being who would reside there. I discovered later that the Tibetan Buddhists have a similar concept, which they call a *tulpa*. This is really not much different from the make-believe friend a child creates in her imagination.

Of course creating a mental golem is harder to do as an adult. The trick that I have found is that it is easier as an adult to start with imagining a place; that is something most of us can still do with ease, and from there, once you have the place it is much easier to construct the mental golem. I'm not sure why this works, but it seems to have to do with giving the creation a place to live, breathe, and grow just as a character within a book needs a novel to grow.

---

* The memory recall part of the technique, which is incidental to our purposes, involves visualizing any bit of info you wish to recall as being inside the memory palace: It works as an imaginary storage receptacle.

I should say, however, that this is a powerful and potentially dangerous spell. It should be attempted only by folks who are mentally stable because it is a form of allowing yourself to go a little bit crazy—at least according to the rational world's point of view. In doing this spell or exercise, you are breathing life into an imaginary being; you are giving a part of your unconscious autonomy. For that reason you want to think very carefully about what you are going to make, what the being looks like, how it acts, its personality. Do not take this lightly.

How to Create a Mental Golem

Step 1
Construct a memory palace, a vividly imagined place. Your golem is going to need a home, a place of residency.

Step 2
Vividly imagine the mental golem you wish to see. It can be as fanciful or as commonplace as you like. This step is very important; think it over carefully before you begin.

Step 3
Converse with your mental creation. Yes, in effect I am simply talking about talking to yourself—creating a sort of mental puppet or marionette, one that, if you breathe enough life into it,

begins to take on a life of its own. What that creature looks like and even, to a large degree, its habits and personality are initially up to you, but like a writer's characters, eventually it will become autonomous and give replies to questions you ask of it that are quite surprising!

Ask it questions. In the beginning you must provide the answers yourself, because at this stage it is like an imaginary puppet. Also your powers of make-believe have likely dwindled much since childhood. At first the conversations will likely be rather simple, like talking to a primitive form of artificial intelligence. With a bit of practice, however, things will gain momentum. Soon the carefully constructed daemon will come to life.

STEP 4

From here things get interesting!

We live in a world that perceives itself to be rational, with no place for the wild, the mystic, the untamed, the ineffable, the unknowable. But real magic must fly in the face of the rational worldview; therefore it involves driving oneself insane. This can be done in a somewhat careful and safe manner, just as any potentially dangerous activity—from skydiving to driving on the highway—is fairly safe if practiced carefully. The greatest deterrent is not from the dangers but that the society we live in claims there is no use for

the magical and the imaginary; there is nothing of value beyond that which can be seen, touched, and measured in the bright light of day.

Once you have gained access to the realm of imagination, you know it is as real as any physical object. The mental golem is a being that, once you meet, will convince you the imaginary realm is still alive, powerful, and unpredictable. There are still lessons and knowledge to be learned from the beings that live in imagination that are as old and wise as the most ancient of humankind's ideas, stories, and dreams.

> *Two men are sitting in a railway car; one of them carries an exotic-looking basket. "I have a mongoose in here," the man explains. "I'm taking it to a friend who is suffering terribly from delirium tremens; the poor fellow sees snakes everywhere." The second man is flabbergasted. "But aren't those imaginary snakes?" he protests. The other man replies, "Of course they are, and this is an imaginary mongoose!"* —An old joke

CONCLUSION

An Irrational Manifesto

A savage hardly conceives the distinction commonly drawn by more advanced peoples between the natural and the supernatural. . . . He, the savage, possesses in himself all the powers necessary to further his own well-being and that of his fellow-men.

—Sir James George Frazer, *The Golden Bough*

Even though we've reached the end, this book is unfinished. Think of each experiment as only a trailhead marker, a beginning. The big question is, What will you do with these tools and new ways of seeing?

I hope that you finish this book and come away with more than a handful of mere tricks and parlor games. This stuff matters—it is the morning of the twenty-first century, and as a species we face tremendous challenges: dire overpopulation, diminishing resources, gross wealth inequality, and a threatened global environment, at risk from what we have collectively made. I hardly know which is a more incredible fact, that we have killed off 97 percent of the tigers* in the past century or that the 85 richest people in the world have as much wealth as the 3.5 billion poorest!†

You're thinking, *Yes, I know, it's terrible, but what does that have to do with magic?*

A lot, actually.

It is not enough to say we are going to try to change our actions. The change needs to happen on a deeper level; what's needed are new tools, new ways of seeing, a new vision. Magic can give you a collection of tools for seeing differently, ways that look inward, not outward, ways that use intuition instead of reason, ways that look toward the soul instead of the surface. While the exercises are simple, new ways of seeing change the way we see ourselves connected to the world and everybody else in it. Magical thinking matters because it is a deeper way of looking at everything.

There was a time when humankind felt connected to the community; when we saw animals as more than just resources to be translated into money or food; when we were connected to the rhythms of nature, the wind, the rain, the mountains, the plains,

---

* Wild tigers are expected to go extinct within eight years.

† That is 50 percent of the world's population. Half! Meanwhile, you could fit eighty-five people on a school bus. It would be a very luxurious school bus, I am sure.

the harvest, and the hunt. That world, we are now told, doesn't matter because it doesn't exist.

Today, there exists an imbalance between our rational side and our irrational, or intuitive, side. When we look at the world through just the lens of the eyes, it is easy to just see you and me, merely a world of individuals. When we look at the world through our other faculties—through spirit, through the heart, through dreams, intuition, magic, and soul—we see we are all a part of the one whole.

We must remember the beauty of things beyond their monetary value. We must remember what it is like to be a soul in a world of souls, to live in a magical world, where all that you can see and touch is only the surface.

This is not an easy way to see; it is a forgotten way, one not found except by the curious and those who seek. It is a way of portals, of fairy tales, and of forgotten lore. It is a way of looking at things differently, of allowing yourself to try things that seem a little bit weird, a little bit scary, a little strange and unusual, a way of listening to the inside as much as to the outside. It is not a way that rejects outright the physical world for the immaterial. Instead, it is a way that seeks to respect both the world and the soul.

The truth of human experience is so much wondrously larger than just that which we can see and touch with our five senses. As I hope these exercises have reminded you, the world is also made from dreaming, and things seen only in starlight, and there are as many emotions as there are hues of visible color: There is love and there is mystery, and they are as real as the ocean and the moon. The whole of reality is greater than the sum of its parts.

By listening to the creative, inner-dreaming soul, magical side of things, we can move forward to a balance that takes into account our two halves—the rational side of the builder, the maker, the merchant, and the statesman, and the other side of the dreamer, the singer, the poet, the prophet, the magus. The poet and the astronomer speak of the same stars, and both agree that we are made of stardust.

ACKNOWLEDGMENTS

First and foremost, thank you to all of the artists who contributed such incredible and cool art to *D.I.Y. Magic*; I am a huge fanboy of each and every one of you. I am also endlessly grateful to Jason Leivian, proprietor of Floating World comics, for curating all of the fantastic illustrations that went into making *D.I.Y. Magic*; this book would not have been written without his help. I would like to thank my amazing agent, Molly Glick, for seeing the potential in this wild and weird bag of ideas, and my wonderful and savvy editor, Meg Leder, for shaping this collection of strange things into a coherent book. Thank you, Amanda Shih, for all of your insightful and patient advice. Big thanks to Jay Babcock for originally running some of these essays in *Arthur*. I'd also like to thank Farel Dalrymple for the encouragement, and the Sou'wester Lodge for the solitude.

FURTHER READING

Ka by Roberto Calasso

Journey to Ixtlan by Carlos Castaneda

The Phenomenon of Man by Pierre Teilhard de Chardin

Aurélia by Gérard de Nerval

Collected Works by Philip K. Dick

Shamanism by Mircea Eliade

The Golden Bough by Sir James Frazer

Dostoevsky by André Gide

Blink by Malcolm Gladwell

The Art of Seduction by Robert Greene

The Secret Teachings of All Ages by Manly P. Hall

The Way of the Shaman by Michael Harner

Daimonic Reality by Patrick Harpur

How to Be Idle by Tom Hodgkinson

Gödel, Escher, Bach by Douglas Hofstadter

I Ching

The Origin of Consciousness in the Breakdown of the Bicameral Mind by Julian
    Jaynes

Memories, Dreams, Reflections by Carl Jung

Further Reading

The Changing Light at Sandover by James Merrill

From Hell by Alan Moore

The Secret Life of Puppets by Victoria Nelson

Anything by Plato

Cartoon Utopia by Ron Rege Jr.

The Duino Elegies by Rainer Maria Rilke

The Illuminations by Arthur Rimbaud

My Idea of Fun by Will Self

The Essential Rumi translated by Coleman Barks

Walden by Henry David Thoreau

The Velveteen Rabbit by Margery Williams

ART CREDITS

Artwork curated by Jason Leivian

Page 2: copyright © by Lala Albert.

Pages 8 and 227: copyright © by Jason Traeger.

Page 14: copyright © by Farel Dalrymple.

Pages 20, 78, 83, and 127: copyright © by Christian Defilippo.

Page 26: copyright © by Jason McLean and Billy Young.

Page 30: copyright © by Jennifer Parks.

Page 37: copyright © by Kevin Hooyman.

Page 41: copyright © by Edie Fake.

Pages 47 and 164: copyright © by Amy Kuttab.

Pages 49, 192, and 181: copyright © by Iñes Estrada.

Pages 55 and 63: copyright © by Aidan Koch.

Pages 67 and 97: copyright © by Nick D'Auria.

Pages 71 and 74: copyright © by Jesse Moynihan.

Pages 88 and 174: copyright © by Maureen Gubia.

Pages 94, 144, 159, 193, 197, and 200: copyright © by Frederic Coche.

Pages 101 and 120: copyright © by Ron Rege Jr.

Pages 108 and 221: copyright © by Conor Stechschulte.

Page 112: copyright © by Marijpol.

Page 117: copyright © by Luke Ramsey.

Art Credits

Page 132: copyright © by Austin English.

Page 138: copyright © by Ian MacEwan.

Page 147: copyright © by Panayiotis Terzis.

Page 153: copyright © by Julia Gförer.

Page 170: copyright © by Pete Toms.

Pages 185, 210, and 242: copyright © by Dunja Jankovic.

Page 190: copyright © by Tommi Musturi.

Page 214: copyright © by Eric Mast.

Page 231: copyright © by Malachi Ward.

Page 237: copyright © by PMurphy.

Page 248: copyright © by Pippi Zornoza.

INDEX

Page numbers in *italics* indicate photos or illustrations and those followed by "n" indicate notes.

Index

Index

Index

Index

Index

Index

Index

Index

Index

ABOUT THE AUTHOR

Anthony Alvarado lives in Portland, Oregon, and spends his time writing when he is not busy daydreaming.